D1527866

*The Enlightenment against
the Baroque*

Jean-Baptiste Pigalle, *Funerary Monument of Maréchal de Saxe*, engraving by Cochin the younger and N. Dupuis. (Bibliothèque nationale, Paris.)

Rémy G. Saisselin

The Enlightenment against the Baroque

Economics and Aesthetics
in the Eighteenth Century

University of California Press

Berkeley   Los Angeles   Oxford

University of California Press
Berkeley and Los Angeles, California

University of California Press, Ltd.
Oxford, England

© 1992 by
The Regents of the University of California

Library of Congress Cataloging-in-Publication Data

Saisselin, Rémy G. (Rémy Gilbert), 1925–
    The Enlightenment against the Baroque : economics and aesthetics
in the eighteenth century / Rémy Saisselin.
        p.   cm.   —   (Quantum books)
    Includes bibliographical references and index.
    ISBN 0-520-07295-2 (alk. paper)
    1. Europe—Civilization—18th century.   2. Civilization, Baroque.
3. Enlightenment.   I. Title.
CB411.S23   1992
940.2'53—dc20   91-24107

Printed in the United States of America
9   8   7   6   5   4   3   2   1

Contents

Introduction

In his *Art as Experience,* John Dewey calls Dr. Johnson a
philistine and questions the sacrosanct aesthetics of Kant.
This assessment makes it possible for us to see the Enlightenment and the eighteenth century in terms other than those
which have long prevailed in aesthetics, in art history, and
in literary history. In aesthetics, on the standard view, everything led to Kant; in art history, everything presumably
moved from the Rococo to the French Revolution; in literature, everything moved from French classicism or English neoclassicism to romanticism. Everything, as the politicians so often say, was thus *moving forward.* Likewise in
economics: everything moved toward Adam Smith and
free trade. Significantly, too, it was during the eighteenth
century that aesthetics, art history, and economics became
autonomous disciplines, while in literature the canons of the
nineteenth century were coming into being.

   Is it possible that this nearly parallel rise of aesthetics and
economics was not pure chance but somehow represents a
linked development, the result of some cause external to
both aesthetics and economics? Perhaps Kant was not the
last word in aesthetics, and art historians have been as much
bewitched by language as have philosophers.

   Take the preposition *to* when put between the two terms
Rococo and *Revolution.* The three words epitomize an interpretation not only of history but of art history, which can

be illustrated by the order of pictures in books or of art
works in a museum exhibition. One reads or moves *from*
"rococo" pictures and artefacts *to* the pictures and artefacts
of the Revolution. Art moves. Art develops. Art even
progresses—from antiquity to the Middle Ages to the Renaissance to the Baroque to the Rococo to neoclassicism to
romanticism to realism to impressionism to postimpres-
sionism to whatever name one may wish to assign to the
production of aesthetic objects today. Words predispose the
minds of art historians as much as do the pictures they look
at, for words, institutions, existing histories, exhibitions,
presuppositions, and prejudices prearrange the materials of
art history in a sequence. Art students in dimly lit class-
rooms are thus enabled to follow slide projections in linear
order from the beginning of art to the present in numbered
courses. There may of course be variations on this linear
scheme. One may pick out themes; one may concentrate on
styles. One may argue over the names of styles. Nevertheless, what has been called the Whig, or progressive,
interpretation of history has been applied to art history as
well, and it is for this reason that the history of the arts in
the eighteenth century can be written as a movement from
Rococo *to* Revolution. Presumably this represents progress.
A monarchist might conceivably have an entirely different
point of view: that neoclassicism, in retrospect, was the
taste of the upstart nouveaux riches. Or one might accept
the terminology of the eighteenth century itself, and consider the Rococo as the truly modern and revolutionary
style and neoclassicism as reactionary—in which case "art"
will be seen to have moved not forward but backward.

But this brings up the question of "art." Perhaps, in
talking about art in the Rococo, we are not talking about
something called "art" at all but about something else, a
multiplicity of specific objects? The term *Rococo* as a style
designation covers a great many things: chairs, couches,
tables, clocks, chests, desks, bidets, powder boxes, pot-
pourris, spinets, violins, coaches, hunting rifles, micro-

scopes, busts, portraits, paintings, statues, drawings, bindings, prints, bibelots, vases, inkwells, etc. All of these have somehow become "art." Dewey's answer to this paradox was to subsume these diverse objects under a single designation. This approach was suggested to him by the peculiar status of art in the United States, as something divorced from experience. All these objects were art because they were in museums. What they all had in common, in addition to the fact of being assembled in collections, was presumably some essence called art or beauty. Art, the word itself, has thus long rested on the essentialist fallacy.

The result is a major difficulty in defining terms such as *Baroque, Rococo, neoclassicism, romanticism,* or *Enlightenment.* The definitions usually involve the linking of certain objects to the words; but the words may mean different things in different countries, and sometimes in different arts. Thus neoclassicism in art as concerns England is not exactly the same thing as English neoclassical literature, and the complications are compounded by crossing the border to Germany or France. Yet the words are there, and they are used—in art history, in literary history, in aesthetics, in cultural history, and even in economics, since there exists a body of writings referring to a classical economics.

In what follows, these terms, with the exception of neoclassicism, will be used not in a purely art historical sense, as referring only to an architectural style or a decorative system, but as period designations for historical moments in Western culture. Thus, in using the term *Baroque,* we mean to designate not only the architecture of Bernini and Borromini, or an open pictorial space and the contrast of light and dark, but a civilization that can be associated with the period of absolute monarchy, with an alliance of church and state to maintain the hierarchical structure of society, and even with economic mercantilism. For this reason we include the age of Louis XIV, which the French see as their "classicism," as still within the Baroque moment because of nonclassical traits belonging to such a moment—the court, religious enthusiasm and mysticism, strong passions, and a conception of the hero, the courtier, and the saint as dominant types. Indeed, French classicism may be interpreted as a tension between a will to order, clarity, and discipline on the one hand, and an unruly and fantastic imagination, religious fanaticism, undisciplined passions, and a dispersal of personality on the other, a tension which in the course of the early seventeenth century made for a general crisis of society.

In view of this use of the word *Baroque,* the term *Rococo,* often distinguished from Baroque by art historians, is considered here as a *diminuendo* Baroque. We have used it to designate the early eighteenth century in France, the age of Madame de Pompadour and Louis XV. In its own time the Rococo was referred to as the modern style, a characterization that neatly distinguishes it from the later manner of style, the neoclassical, which in France was referred to as the *retour à l'antique.* As employed here, the term *Rococo* is thus still within the Baroque moment. The Baroque did not die with a change in the design of furniture or with the triumph of David, but with the end of a certain society. The arrival of a new style may herald changes within a society even while the society still seems securely established; likewise a style may persist in one cultural sphere even while in others a new one is being elaborated. Thus, while England and France were going neoclassical in architecture and interior decor, Bavarian churches were still in the late Baroque, the "Rococo." To sum up the situation in France and our use of the two terms *Baroque* and *Rococo,* a Louis XV armchair in the room in which it stood about 1740 was then considered in the "modern manner." We call it rococo; yet that so-called rococo chair in 1740 stood within a cultural milieu which was still baroque. On the other hand, a Louis XVI chair, based on Etruscan or Roman models, was in its day considered to be *à l'ancienne* or in the antique manner, the *goût antique,* which we call neoclassical. This style, the neoclassical, heralded a mentality which was no longer baroque, even if the court at Versailles made no connection between a changed style and a new mentality which was emerging beyond the château and the park. But does the emergence of a neoclassical style in architecture and interior decor mean that the neoclassical style was that of the Enlightenment, manifested as an anti-baroque mentality?

In fact it is only very recently that the term *Enlightenment* has come to be associated with the neoclassical style. The reason is clear, but no less wrong for all that: the Enlightenment is associated with the modern state, with republics and parliamentary regimes, and modern regimes are architecturally represented not by palaces in the baroque style but by white houses in the Palladian manner, public buildings built on the classical orders and banks and supreme court buildings along the same neoclassical lines. One tends to forget that these neoclassical buildings were often designed before the Enlightenment had been translated into the institutions of modern states. In Russia, neoclassical architecture is that of absolute monarchy; in France it became that of the republic, as in the United States; in Prussia it was the architecture of an efficient monarchy; later it would also become the architecture of totalitarian states. We shall therefore use the term *neoclassicism* only to designate a style, not an entire civilization as with the word *Baroque*. And the term *Enlightenment* will not be applied to art, but to a mentality opposed to the Baroque: a pan-European intellectual-critical movement advocating religious tolerance, economic liberalism, modernization of the state, judicial and fiscal reform, and a revaluation of human nature in terms of a more optimistic and secular view of the destiny of man. Implicit here is a metaphysics founded not so much on rationalism as on nature and empiricism, and a psychology based less on the baroque notion of the passions than on the sensationalism of Locke and Condillac.

It is our view that this Enlightenment mentality, as manifest in its analysis and criticism of the arts, society, and religion, made it possible to separate what in the Baroque had been perceived as united: art, society, religion, morality, mores, in brief, the baroque assumption of the conjunction of reality and appearance. The enlightened mind penetrated appearances to reveal the fictions of baroque society, and so drew distinctions between art and luxury, taste and fashion, morality and aesthetics, subject and object. If for Shakespeare all the world was a stage, for Fontenelle the universe was a stage to create illusions which the enlightened mind saw as such because it knew how the stage machinery operated to produce those illusions. A society built on the concept of art gave way to one constructed on concepts derived from natural science.

1

Pascal's Room, Mandeville's Bees, and Baroque Spending

"I have learned," wrote Pascal, "that all the unhappiness of men comes from one single thing, which is that they do not know how to remain at rest in a room" (*Pensées*, no. 139). For man without grace is anxious, restless, subject to ennui, and the prey of his all-too-human and corrupted nature, *omne animal*. Pascal's room, however, was not Sartre's *huis clos*, that room with no exit in which men and women, born free—indeed, in Sartre's terms, condemned to be free—torture each other endlessly. There was a door in Pascal's room, and one might leave it to seek grace or diversion, *divertissement*. There were three roads one might take after leaving the room: the narrow path of the Jansenist doctrine of grace, the far more easy and agreeable road proposed by the Jesuits, or the road to court and town in search of glory, pleasure, riches, or some moderate manner of life made bearable by wisdom and philosophy. This third road was that of *divertissement* from one's own self and one's ennui; it was the road of worldly ambition, dominated not so much by Providence as by *Fortuna*. It was, one might also say, the road of Dr. Mandeville's bees.

Dr. Bernard Mandeville, a native of Holland who lived and wrote in Augustan England, is a puzzling figure made famous by his doggerel poem *The Fable of the Bees* (1714). Its notes clarified the moral—the amoral moral—of the poem, to the effect that private vices made for public benefits. This was a doctrine at odds both with the civic humanist tradition linking private and public virtue and with Christian morality. Even later economists disapproved; for, being rationalists, they could hardly be expected to appreciate paradox and accept a characterization of what they saw as productive forces, improvement of living conditions, and initiative as being the result of private vices.

Mandeville puzzles us less than he did his own contemporaries, for not only are we post-Enlightenment and post-bourgeois but we also live in what is characterized as a consumer society. If he seems paradoxical, it may be because he belonged both to a passing world and to one in the making but not yet clearly delineated. His allusions to Montaigne and Bayle place him within a well-established tradition of skepticism, a tradition closer to Christian pessimism than to a latitudinarian Christianity accommodating itself to the ways of the world. To the Jansenists and other austere Christian sects, the world was largely evil and salvation was to be sought elsewhere. Mandeville's poem might thus be seen as a satire on those who would accommodate Christian morality with the world, or perhaps on those who would have all men be virtuous, moral, and righteous.

In truth Mandeville is very much of his time, the Baroque. He points clearly to what can be called baroque spending, divertissement, and glory, and to the view prevalent in the Baroque that men are driven by passions rather than by reason, thoughts of virtue, or generosity; thus man without grace, or without culture, is an animal. Mandeville's view of man is not without affinities to that of Hobbes or that of the Spanish moralist Baltasar Gracián, who thought man is born a barbarian and can rise to true humanity only through culture. Society is possible only because men have been persuaded by clever lawgivers to give up real and immediate advantages for "imaginary" rewards such as honor, glory, the reputation for virtue, civic distinctions, and praise. The social world is thus a cloak hiding the beast beneath it, which explains the baroque's preoccupation with appearances, masks, and a psychology aimed at unveiling the true motives of men beneath the appearances of affability, civility, charm, and manners. Mandeville's poem and his copious notes to it, as later Rousseau's discourses and other writings, lifted the various masks invented by and for society.

Men had learned to live in society; but their nature had not changed. If for Pascal it was ennui that lay at the heart of man, for Mandeville it was pride. The state of society did not eliminate passions; and Mandeville's view of man was thus no different from that expressed by Candide as he and Martin sailed toward France:

> "Do you think," said Candide, "that men have always massacred each other, as they do today? Have they always been liars, cheats, traitors, brigands, weak, flighty, cowardly, envious, gluttonous, drunken, grasping, and vicious, bloody, backbiting, debauched, fanatical, hypocritical and silly?" "Do you think," said Martin, "that sparrow-hawks have always eaten the pigeons they came across?" (290)

Mandeville's paradox lies in his demonstration that these vices ultimately add up to a general prosperity. Consider, for example, prodigality:

> Was it not for prodigality, nothing could make us amends for the rapine and extortion of avarice in power. When a covetous statesman is gone, who spent his whole life in fattening himself with the spoils of the nation and had by pinching and plundering heaped up an immense treasure, it ought to fill every good member of the society with joy to behold the

uncommon profuseness of his son. This is refunding
to the public what was robbed from it. (75)

This argument was later used by Diderot to explain the
function of the mistresses of the financiers, and on a higher
level it was also used, as we shall see, to justify luxury
spending. It was certainly not a very moral point of view;
Hogarth did not look on his *Rake's Progress* with the same
eye as that of Mandeville. Nor was it to be the view of the
later economists, either the Physiocrats or Adam Smith and
his adherents. The important point is that Mandeville is here
concerned with spending rather than production, and the
vice of prodigality rather than the virtue of frugality, which
he dismisses:

> Frugality is like honesty, a mean starving virtue, that
> is only fit for small societies of good peaceable men,
> who are contented to be poor, so they may be easy
> but, in a large stirring nation, you may have soon
> enough of it. It is an idle dreaming virtue that employs
> no hands, and therefore very useless in a trading coun-
> try, where there are vast numbers that one way or
> other must all be set to work. Prodigality has a thou-
> sand inventions to keep people from sitting still that
> frugality would never think of. (75–76)

Mandeville puzzled austere Christian moralists as well as
those in the tradition of neo-Stoicism. He did not puzzle
Voltaire, whose poem *Le Mondain* celebrates luxury and
therefore civilization rather than the state of nature and the
much-vaunted frugal and simple ways of the ancient Romans. Mandeville's paradoxes about the beneficial aspects
of what were considered human vices point to the baroque
solution for Pascal's restless man: the ennui and anxiety of
the soul may be dispelled by prodigality as well as divertissement. Thus Pascal and Mandeville both point to two
related developments of the eighteenth century: the appearance of economics and of aesthetics as autonomous areas of

inquiry. Pascal's true successor is the abbé Du Bos, whose aesthetic derives from the Pascalian notion of divertisse-ment, while the successors and critics of Mandeville are the Physiocrats and Adam Smith. Du Bos's aesthetic of taste and pleasure is as baroque as Mandeville's apology for prod-igality.

But with the Physiocrats and the new morality of the philosophes and encyclopedists, such as Rousseau and Di-derot, a new aesthetic arose to challenge that of Mandeville and Du Bos, one implying a new economics as well. It spelled the end of the Baroque as an era in which the aes-thetic and the economic were inextricably mixed—a time when gold was specie as well as plate, exchange value as well as beauty, but sometimes also mere false glitter.

The false glitter was perceived and exposed by another moralist. La Bruyère also pondered upon the confusion of the economic and the aesthetic as well as the relation of money to the nobility. In his classic *Caractères,* which first appeared in 1687, La Bruyère looked at court and town, the great and the rich, and saw mostly appearances belying what lay behind them. As one of his recent exegetists, Doris Kirsch, writes: "Instead of considering the privileges and refined exteriors of the courtesans as symbols of their 'gra-tuitous superiority,' La Bruyère . . . sees in them a paid and paying superiority measured solely in terms of material advantage" (*La Bruyère, ou le style cruel,* 133). The finding is amply illustrated by current historical research on the wealth, status, privileges, and finances of the nobility of the ancien régime; La Bruyère indeed unmasks the society of his time. Kirsch goes on to an even more telling conclusion:

In the *Caractères,* the two fundamental aspects of court life are no longer conformity to tradition and pleasure, which had historically defined worldly morality; they are, rather, conditioning and consumption, the two characteristics which mark the advent of modern bourgeois society. From La Bruyère's perspective the luxury of the privileged class can no longer be defined

as liberty or an aesthetic pleasure, but has on the
contrary become a constraint, an activity of consuming, and even a necessity of which the aristocracy was
prisoner.

La Bruyère saw the same thing that Mandeville and others
saw at the time, but his perspective was different: where
Mandeville concentrated on the social effects of luxury, La
Bruyère focused on moral truth and individual wisdom.
The eighteenth century, one might venture, resolved the
opposition between dissipation and morality, spending and
frugality, sin and virtue, Mammon and God, by disentan-
gling the economic from the aesthetic, thinking thereby to
purify both through the moralization of spending and the
naturalization of the aesthetic.

•   •   •

The difference between baroque spending and the new
attitude to prodigality, a stance implying a new economics
as well as a new aesthetics, can be exemplified with reference to gardens. These, like metaphysical systems, may
be taken as paradigms of society's ideological assumptions.
The formal gardens of Le Nôtre are pure art and pure
expense, having only a metaphysical relation to nature.
The formal garden—with its clipped hedges and shaped
trees, its expanse, its multishaped, geometric parterres, ba-
sins, fountains, pools, and water mirrors, its *allées,* circles,
and statues, and its picnics and festivals or fireworks, with
music and dancing and the appearance of king and court—
presupposes a metaphysical distinction between a crude,
given, empirical nature, and a purer, superior, intellectual,
systematized, generalized nature. Such gardens might indeed be spoken of in connection with Descartes's universe,
though they were being designed even as he was building
up that universe. Such gardens are the gardens of the king,
of princes and great lords, and they are the result of immense expense. Prodigality and all its effects are plain to

see here, for not only architects, sculptors, and mechanics but also armies of workers and gardeners were kept busy.

We can borrow from contemporary financial jargon the notion of cash flow to distinguish between baroque and nonbaroque spending. In fact, amusingly enough, water-works were among the most expensive features of the formal gardens: cash flow in the baroque, when not used for war, was water flow. At Versailles, where there was no water to begin with, the consumption costs of water and maintenance of the waterworks were immense, even though the fountains were not kept on continually but were reserved for special occasions. In 1678, some 821,000 livres were allotted for the parks and gardens. The following year the costs had risen to 965,000 livres, and by 1680 to 1,627,000 livres. Four years later work on an aqueduct to bring more water to the gardens and ponds cost an additional 1,143,000 livres, while hundreds of thousands were spent on an elaborate machine erected at Marly to pump water uphill from the Seine to the king's ever-thirsty gardens. The water was for spectacle.

But there were other expenses once the initial reconfiguration of the site was concluded. It cost 200,000 livres in 1668–69 just to dig the first basin for the grand canal complex with its flotilla of nine pleasure boats. In 1671, 696,000 livres were allotted to extend and broaden the grand canal, with an additional 264,000 required in 1672. Further, once the gardens were constructed they had to be planted, and at the Grand Trianon the parterres required, according to Le Nôtre's calculations, two million flowerpots. The parterres, like the waters, had to please the eye, and so pots with wilting or dried-out flowers were changed daily. It is significant that by the reign of Louis XV this expense could no longer be borne; one could look back nostalgically to a time when one could afford nine hundred thousand pots at Trianon and a daily change of wilting flowers.

By contrast the landscape gardens of the type "improved" by Capability Brown implied not only a different aesthetic, based on a different metaphysics of nature, but also a new economics. Not that they were inexpensive; rather, they looked inexpensive because they looked as if they *were* nature, and nature was bountiful. In the baroque scheme of things, bullion might be converted into flowing water, cascades, spouts, water mirrors, and water theater. In the Enlightenment scheme, bullion was thought better applied to agricultural improvement, trade, and manufacturing. Beauty was perceived less in what artists had called the "general nature," or the "ideal nature," the model of the classical landscape painters, than in the given, empirical, experienced nature, a piece of land which might be improved so as to yield not only a truer beauty but also an increased net product. When Arthur Young traveled through France, he not only commented on the state of agriculture but also experienced a new form of aesthetic pleasure associated with a flourishing agriculture and the beauty of tilled fields, rich orchards, the regularity of well-tended vineyards, well-kept farms, and well-cut hedges—in short, the prosperity of the land. By then the old aesthetic built on the notion of ideal nature, or art, taste, and luxury, had been relegated to the sphere of critical inquiry. The beautiful had changed, and so had economics. This does not preclude the writing of a history of art or aesthetics separate from that of economics. But such separate histories could only arise once luxury had been separated from art on the conceptual level.

Art or Luxury?

When one writes about the arts today one does so, willy-nilly, under the often unstated influence of Kant and the nineteenth-century notion of Art with a capital A. Art is art and luxury is luxury. Any art dealer will tell you that art is beyond price—which of course is why flowers by Van Gogh may go for millions on the auction block. And because of museums, art is part of culture, and in museums what was once considered luxury turns into art. Art is thus connected with the aesthetic, while luxury is connected with money.

But before Kant and before the museums, the line between luxury and art was far from clear, and neither was clearly differentiated from the manner of life permitted by baroque spending and prompted by pride and ennui. Mandeville reminds us that what we call a style is also a way of life:

> The worldly-minded, voluptuous, and ambitious man, notwithstanding he is void of merit, covets precedence everywhere and desires to be dignified above his betters. He aims at spacious palaces and delicious gardens; his chief delight is in excelling others in stately horses, magnificent coaches, a numerous attendance, the dear-bought furniture. To gratify his lust, he wishes for genteel, young, beautiful women of different charms and complexions that shall adore his greatness, and be really in love with his person. His cellars he would have stored with the flower of every country that produces excellent wines; his table he desires may be served with many courses, and each of them contain a choice variety of dainties not easily purchased, and ample evidences of elaborate and judicious cookery; while harmonious music and well-couched flattery entertain his hearing by turns. . . . He desires to have several sets of witty, facetious, and polite people to converse with, and among them he would have some famous for learning and universal knowledge. (104)

What is being described here, in all the richness of its multiple pleasures, is the noble life. The very use of the word *noble* bestows upon this lifestyle an aura which makes one forget that it rests on mere money and not necessarily on merit. La Bruyère and Mandeville are at one in this baroque turn of mind and in their observation of their contemporaries, just as both saw a tendency at work, already in their own time, to sublimate mere riches. For, continues Mandeville, this same rich man living this noble life would have the world believe that his life is a burden he must bear, and that what really matters are the higher things of life and the public good. Conventional wisdom has it that spiritual values are superior to dependence on material goods, and that self-reliance, self-denial, and a contented and serene mind are the true virtues of this world. But Mandeville could not quite believe, any more than Pascal or La Bruyère, that the world acted according to this conventional wisdom. They believed the evidence of their eyes: "How can I believe that a man's chief delight is in the embellishment of the mind when I see him ever employed about and daily pursue the pleasures that are contrary to them?" (107). Mandeville thus points not only to man's pride and pretensions, but to the prevalence of Pascalian divertissement. The noble life is the love of luxury and pleasure, not the sign of some superior quality or merit.

This skeptical attitude renders impossible an aesthetic which would sublimate luxury into art, spiritualize riches, and elevate the noble life to an object of admiration. La Bruyère's attitude toward collectors, connoisseurs, and the *curieux* is as negative as his view of the great, the courtesans, and the rich. Men of taste, antiquarians, are not men of particularly noble passions, and are more likely to be followers of fashion than lovers of true beauty or true quality.

Neither La Bruyère nor Mandeville thus singles out the "virtuoso" for praise, as would Shaftesbury in his *Characteristics*. If La Bruyère's style can be called one of cruelty, then Shaftesbury's is that of noble generosity. It is through him that the man of taste would eventually be seen as something more than a mere seeker after divertissement and connoisseur of luxuries and pleasures. For Shaftesbury represents precisely the type alluded to by Mandeville: a believer in the superiority of spiritual goods over material and worldly goods and pleasures. But that belief could not be justified without separating luxury from art and rigorously distinguishing the economic from the aesthetic.

•   •   •

When the abbé Du Bos looked about him while writing his *Réflexions critiques sur la poésie et la peinture,* which was published in 1719, five years after Mandeville's *Bees,* he saw much the same thing as had Mandeville. But he took the argument further, and laid the foundations for a distinction between luxury and art. With the ancient Greeks in mind he wrote: "The works of the great masters were not looked upon, in the times of which I speak, as ordinary furniture destined to embellish the apartment of some private individual. They were reputed the jewels of a State and a public treasure, the enjoyment of which was owed to all citizens" (176). The distinction would not be lost on the philosophes. For Du Bos's contemporaries, however, the line between art and luxury remained blurred—though this did not prevent the development of a sophisticated poetics, a therapeutic view of the function of comedy and tragedy, a theory of the passions in the arts, and the insight that over the course of history the arts have risen and fallen in conjunction with the general prosperity of a society. Du Bos's remark, however, does point to the preponderance of luxury in his own time as contrasted with other historical eras, and more precisely with the four great moments of western civilization—the Age of Pericles, of Augustus, of Leo X, and of Louis XIV. From this historical perspective, the great moments of art in the past stood in contrast to the all-too-obvious reign of money and luxury in 1719. Historical perspective created an aesthetic illusion in a present which seemed all divertissement and luxury.

If today we do not see things quite the way Du Bos did, it is in part because of Kant, as stated above, but also because the furniture Du Bos alluded to is now to be seen in museums, and what is in museums is ipso facto "art." But consider a masterpiece contemporary with the publishing of the *Réflexions critiques: Gersaint's Sign,* by Watteau. It is, for us, a prized masterwork reproduced in books of art history. In its time it was commissioned as a sign for a picture dealer. One did not commission "art," one commissioned specific types of pictures for specific purposes and designated spaces. Watteau, being Watteau, outdid himself in the case of Gersaint's commission, and painted a sign which could hardly be hung outside the dealer's shop. But in doing so he gives us a most telling view of the status of "art" in the early eighteenth century. Watteau's painting depicts a view into a luxury shop. The pictures within the picture, seen hanging on the wall, are not in the grand manner but in the *petite manière,* or *goût moderne,* and appear in elaborate and highly decorative frames ready to be sold as luxury items to decorate some private person's apartment—precisely as Du Bos said. The grand manner, art associated with magnificence, with the court or the church, is also represented, by a picture of Louis XIV; it is being packed off, as a lady looks on and her escort beckons her not to linger over the old king. For the escort, as for the viewer of the picture, the center of attention is the group of amateurs or *curieux* looking at a landscape in an oval frame, while another group is examining a mirror, a small picture, or some jewelry at a counter. We are looking at an art market inseparable from the luxury trade. The *marchands-merciers* of the rue Saint-Honoré who catered to court and town sold not only pictures and delicate furniture, but also jewelry, miniatures, watches, and bibelots.

To us this is the Rococo, and we tend to consider this period in terms of style and the givens of art history and aesthetics. But in its own time, as indicated by the testimony of Du Bos, Mandeville, and Shaftesbury, the age was one of luxury, and from the point of view of economic history it partook of the luxury capitalism described by Werner Sombart or the way of life of the privileged consuming class discussed by Herbert Lüthy. And, historical distinctions between Rococo and Baroque notwithstanding, it also partook of baroque spending. Stylistically and historically one may associate baroque art with the Church, the palace, and the court, with the propagation of the faith and the magnificence of monarchical power. In this case Rococo may be considered as baroque in the private sector, the Baroque of the town and the *hôtel particulier* and even the *petite maison,* of the feminine and the rich. And the latter meant, at that time, the financier class.

The Rococo is thus the feminine moment of the Baroque. After the baroque hero and his high worth, after the moment of spirituality and martyrdom with its spiritualized sensuality (witness Bernini), the Rococo represented a more mundane moment in which at times the flesh seemed to triumph over the spirit. It was not for nothing that Stendhal thought the eighteenth century the age of *amour-goût.* As the age of metaphysics yielded gradually to that of sensationalism in philosophy, so in the private sphere the sensual, the pretty, the light-colored, the gilt overcame the more somber, sublime, noble, and spiritual images of the Baroque.

Had the designation *style Pompadour* caught on outside France as well as it did within it, a great deal of confusion as to how to define and distinguish the Rococo from the Baroque might have been avoided. The Marquise de Pompadour is emblematic of the "Rococo moment," as Winckelmann is of the later eighteenth century, and she certainly deserves as much attention from cultural historians and aestheticians as does Winckelmann, even if she did not write treatises on beauty or the imitation of ancient art. For the two not only represent the contrast and the essential difference between two styles of art, but also two essentially different attitudes toward the arts and spending in the arts. They epitomize the difference between art for life and life for art. But it is also the difference between the stance of the patron of the arts and the purely aesthetic attitude of the collector and scholar.

Madame de Pompadour was a woman of taste, excellent manners, and education (of the kind then given to women who were destined for the higher circles of society). She was trained from her youth on to play a role at court, and as such was a woman of action. Winckelmann was a scholar, a librarian, a cicerone, a convert to Catholicism, and an enthusiast of ancient art. He was an aesthete *avant la lettre* whose imagination turned to the beauty of the past with a corresponding disdain for the works of the present, indeed dismissing most of baroque art as a deviation from the true taste and beauty defined by the Greeks.

Madame de Pompadour was no aesthete but a woman of the world, for whom the arts were a means to perfecting the noble style of life in the present. In this sense she was not a romantic, whereas Winckelmann's love of ancient Greece was already a romantic sentiment, a nostalgia heralding the poetry of Hölderlin or Keats. The Winckelmannian ideal and his vision and projection of ancient Greece may thus have been a creative force for romanticism, but as regards the visual arts they were productive rather of antiquomania, antiquarian studies, and ultimately the academic doctrine of the classical ideal as the supreme and only valid standard of taste in the production of painting and sculpture. This was not the self-imposed discipline of true classicism such as obtained in the Renaissance and the Baroque, the creation of order in the face of tendencies toward disorder, disintegration, exaggeration, multiplicity, and unbounded imagination, but rather a *neo*classicism requiring that certain works be imitated and imposing doctrinal standards from outside. The truly revolutionary style of the eighteenth century was not neoclassicism but the modern manner, the *petite manière,* adapted to the requirements of the present and founded on the imagination of artists rather than on doctrines grounded in scholarship and on some supposedly lost ideal of beauty.

The contrast between the two styles and tastes is also illuminating in economic terms. The taste for the antique did call forth new works in the manner of the antique, but within the market of art, as against direct commissions connected to the construction of a new town house or château; it also made for the success of charlatans, middlemen, and dealers and collectors. Indeed, the ancient works were themselves turned into luxury commodities. Winckelmann and others might have written treatises on ancient art as works which in their time were not luxury, but this did not prevent the items themselves, dug up in the eighteenth century and written about and illustrated, from being turned into marketable items—in short, luxuries from the past. As Quatremère de Quincy would point out after the Revolution, the signs of the past had been turned into collectibles.

At least Madame de Pompadour and those who followed her example and surrounded themselves with the comforts and pleasures of the modern manner never had any pretensions of raising their luxuries to the level of an aesthetic or of philosophical discussion. Her taste had no theoretical underpinnings or justification. It was a discernment, a choice, made within the parameters of the arts of her time—a conception of art which was soon to be denied in the name of an ideal beauty of the past by those who knew that past but partially. One can see here the conflict of two opposed eighteenth-century elites: one for whom art is luxury and pleasure in the present; another for whom art is "aesthetic" and distinct from luxury, an art partaking of the essence of a beauty thought of in terms of eternity and universality—luxury opposed to High Art.

Though the background of the Marquise de Pompadour was bourgeois, her education was not. She was destined for higher things. She would never be the compliant bourgeoise, content to remain in her apartment and social station; she could never be a Madame Jourdain, who found it ridiculous of her husband to take on the manners of a gentleman. Through her mother, the mistress of the financier Lenormand de Tournehem, the future marquise was allied to the financial class, a class which was indispensable to court and king and which did not live *bourgeoisement* but *noblement*—for the boundaries between the sword, the *robe,* and finance were rather fluid, with finance taking on more and more luster over the course of the century. With her triumph at court the financial class also triumphed, and once she had risen to the rank of marquise and was recognized as the titled mistress of the king, she spent in a manner to be expected of those in high places. She may have kept excellent accounts, like a good bourgeoise, but like the nobility of the court she overspent. And like a baroque prince she loved buildings and building, and what she did not build she transformed and redecorated. Thus patronage of the arts, in her case, meant not so much collecting works of art as building and decorating, and this meant that the arts—what we call the arts—flourished hand in hand with luxury spending.

She first bought the now all-but-vanished Château de Crécy-Couvé, south of Dreux. The château and adjacent land cost 790,000 livres. But the structure was in need of repair, and for the work required she turned to her favorite architect, Lassurance. Masonry, carpentry, and roofing cost an additional 100,000 livres; the interior decoration, the work of the sculptors J. Rousseau, Verberckt, and Pigalle, amounted to a total of 2,500,000 livres. Maintenance costs were high, too, since considerable personnel were required: one concierge, one chaplain, eight gamekeepers, one doorman, four maids, one valet and decorator, two waiters, one scrubber, two boys to help in the garden. Total wages for all these came to 10,460 livres per year. The marquise had to give up Crécy-Couvé in 1757.

Needless to say there were other châteaux, *petites maisons* in which to relax away from court, and two splendid hôtels —one in Versailles, the Hôtel des Réservoirs, and one in Paris, the Hôtel d'Evreux, now the Elysée. Bellevue was her preferred château, situated at Meudon overlooking the Paris plain and built by Lassurance according to plans by

Gabriel. Eight hundred men worked on it, and she made use of the best talent of the day for the garden sculpture and the interior décor: Pigalle, Oudry, Caffieri, Verberckt, Coustou, Boucher, Van Loo. The château included a theater in the chinoiserie style. It marked the high point of her career and cost her 2,576,000, perhaps more. But here again she was forced to sell, to Louis XV in 1757 for a mere 325,000 livres, because she needed the money to pay off her debts.

She had always overspent, for the pensions she received from the king and through her positions at court were not that high. From 1746 through 1764 she received 977,207 livres, but spent 1,767,687; the difference she made up by gambling and selling off some of her jewelry. All this did not prevent her from distributing a great deal of money to diverse charities, or from promoting and helping to finance the establishment and building of the Ecole Militaire. These charitable expenses were also part of the obligations of baroque spending, and the great did not fail to include the poor in their wills.

The Marquise de Pompadour's prodigality was only the most highly placed example of a type of spending which was imitated by the lesser mistresses of men occupying lesser ranks in society. The most conspicuous spenders were the farmers-general, or tax collectors under the ancien régime, and those occupying lesser posts in that vast and complex bureaucracy which raised revenues for the king's treasury, the army, the navy, and the apparatus of the state. The police reports are eloquent testimony to the spending lavished by this class on their mistresses and pleasures. Bertin de Blagny compromised his fortune by keeping too many mistresses. He spent 18,000 livres on jewelry and 20,000 on dresses for La Testelingue, with two other mistresses to maintain at the same time. He subsequently gave up La Testelingue for an infantry officer's wife, who only cost him 3,000 in furniture. But between 1760 and 1766 the police noted a total of eight more mistresses. Brissart spent perhaps 500,000 on the actress Deschamps; Mlle La Guerre ruined the Duc de Bouillon, after due warning, and also the tax farmer Haudry de Soucy.

The connection between money, luxury, art, and women need hardly be stressed. It was an integral part of the Rococo, pervading taste, manner, style, and divertissement. It was also inseparable from that ennui Pascal had discerned in the human soul. The connection between ennui and the need for divertissement had been noted by Du Bos; the connection between ennui and the life and luxury of the rich was also noted by the sensualist philosophe Helvétius. The search for divertissement, pleasure, and luxury came down in the end to a flight from ennui.

Luxury as Disease

If for Pascal man's fundamental ennui was linked to original sin, for the materialist philosophe Helvétius, author of *De l'esprit* (1758) and the posthumously published *De l'homme* (1772), ennui was a disease of the soul due to an insufficiency of lively sensations. In this analysis Helvétius followed the abbé Du Bos; however, unlike Du Bos and Pascal, he did not think of ennui as a universal condition, but primarily as an affliction of the idle rich. The entire life of the rich and the great, the men and women living in luxury such as Mandeville had described, was thus organized, at least in France, to escape ennui:

> In France . . . a thousand duties of social behavior unknown among other nations have been engendered by boredom. A woman gets married; she gives birth to a child. One of the men of leisure hears of it; he takes it upon himself to make so many calls; goes to her door every day, talks to the doorman; climbs back into his carriage and goes off to be bored somewhere else.
> What is more, this same man of leisure condemns himself each day to so many calling cards, so many

letters of felicitation written in disgust and read the same way.

The man of leisure would like to experience strong sensations at every instant. These alone can tear him from his ennui. Failing these strong sensations, he takes hold of those within reach. I am alone; I light a fire. The fire keeps me company. (*De l'homme*, 4:145)

Helvétius's books were generally condemned, and *De l'homme* was singled out by Diderot for a philosophical refutation. Helvétius's materialism may be rather simple, but as a social commentator he is not without authority. He had been a farmer-general and so had experience of what he was writing about. He knew high society, he knew the world of the financiers, and he was also acquainted with that other focus of the search for sensual gratification, the best brothels of the city. All this imparts added weight to his observations on ennui in his society.

For Helvétius, ennui and the various remedies proposed for it varied according to nations and their constitutions. In Portugal, for example, where the rich and the great had no voice in the affairs of the state and where the Church, or superstition, did not allow them to think, love and jealousy were the sole remedies for ennui. Other societies could have recourse to the reading of novels, amusements of all sorts, the pursuit and seduction of women, or the chase. In some instances, even religious practices might be explained in terms of ennui: the devout life, regular attendance at mass, devotions of all sorts, and frequent communion and confession were all ways of combating boredom. And of course there were the *arts d'agrément,* the "agreeable" or fine arts. Following Du Bos, Helvétius constructs an aesthetic of pleasure based on sensationalism: "The object of art . . . is to please and consequently to excite sensations in us which, without being painful, are yet lively and strong. When a work produces such effects it is applauded" (4:157). Beauty is what strikes us sufficiently to enliven our soul and please us. The sublime makes for stronger effects since it may evoke terror and fear, but even that is better than being bored. But too much beauty, like too much pleasure, soon produces disgust, satiety, and renewed boredom, whence the constant need for variety in one's diversions and pleasures. Depending on the nature of the pleasure sought or given, one may set up a hierarchy of the arts as a hierarchy of genres corresponding more or less to a hierarchy of taste and culture, with burlesque reserved for those of low taste, and tragedy, comedy, or epic for the higher and nobler strata, who can be stimulated to thought as well as feeling. In fact, the classical aesthetic which had ruled the arts since the ancients and which reasserted itself during the Renaissance and the Baroque is not incompatible with the sensationalism of Helvétius or with the social and cultural interpretation of the hierarchy of genres. The arts were to be judged not by the rules of the pedants but by sentiment, which could be explained by sensationalism, while the hierarchy of genres was justified by the social hierarchy. One might read the history of the arts in terms of the development of society, as did Batteux, Montesquieu, and Du Bos; one might also think of the arts in terms of a therapeutic for ennui, as did Pascal, Du Bos, and Helvétius.

Yet, reading Helvétius, one may also infer that he considered the therapeutic to have failed, since the idle rich, enjoying wine, women, and all the pleasures of the arts, were still subject to ennui: "It is in vain that the rich man assembles the pleasurable arts about him: these arts cannot endlessly produce new impressions for him, nor distract him for long from his ennui" (4:187). This failure of the aesthetic of pleasure and divertissement was signaled at about the same time by Voltaire, in the person of the rich and grand Venetian senator Pococurante, whom Martin and Candide call upon as they pass through Venice. Candide thinks him a man of immense superiority because he is so difficult to please amidst his splendor. Martin explains that Pococurante is simply dis-gusted: he has lost all taste for those very things which have been destined to please him. Indeed, Helvétius found it very difficult to amuse the idle rich:

> Nothing is more difficult than to amuse the leisured. They are easily disgusted. And it is this universal disgust [in the sense of loss of taste] which renders leisure such a severe judge of the beauties of the arts and requires such perfection. Were this passive leisure more sensitive and less bored it would be less difficult [to please]. . . . It is in vain that dancing, painting, in short the most voluptuous of the arts, and more specifically arts devoted to love, recall frenzy and rapture; for what effect will they have on those exchausted by enjoyment and blasé about love? If the rich man runs to balls and spectacles, it is only to change his ennui and thereby soften his malaise. (4:188–89)

Happiness thus does not come from the passivity of the soul, but from activity, not from luxuries possessed, but from the acquisition of objects desired, not from twenty million in the bank, but from the activity of acquiring that twenty million. For then the soul is active, or, as the Baroque put it, in motion—occupied, fixed upon an object not possessed but desired, and thus ignorant of ennui.

· · ·

From ennui considered as a disease of the individual soul to ennui as a social disease was but a single step, and luxury was seen as the symptom of the disease, or corruption, of society. And the counterpart of seeing luxury as a disease of society was of course to posit nature as health. Thus luxury, which in the minds of Mandeville, Pascal, and many of the moralists of the Baroque had been an effect of human nature, pride, sin, barbarism, greed—in brief, all human vices—became, in the new, non-Christian, even nonskeptical critique, an aberration from the natural. This rethinking of the natural implied a general critique of appearances—that is, a full-blown critique of baroque society encompassing both economics and the arts. This great change in French thought began about 1750, and its most eloquent spokesman, the most devastating and thorough critic of baroque society in its advanced state of luxury and hence corruption, was the citizen of Geneva, the capital of Protestantism, Jean-Jacques Rousseau. His eloquence was such as to raise the problem to a universal plane. The question of luxury ceased to be a debate between moralists and the nouveaux riches, or between clerics and the rich, or a debate on trade versus landed wealth. Rather, it turned into a debate between nature and society, and thus became a critique of the constituted society and regime. The question involved not only philosophers and philosophes, moralists of the old persuasion, literary critics, the new art critics, and even musical critics, but a totally new type of thinker belonging to a new sect: the economists. It is no coincidence that many of the events and phenomena which will figure in the coming pages—the critique of opera, the famous battle of the buffoons involving an attack on French lyrical drama, or court opera, the rise of art criticism and the critique of court painting, Rousseau's discourses on the arts and the origins of property, the publication of the first volumes of the *Encyclopédie* and the first books of economics, the first critique of baroque architecture by the abbé Laugier, and the publication of Montesquieu's *Esprit des lois*—occur between 1748 and 1755. Those years mark the beginning of the end of the baroque world—an end initiated by a critique of its art forms, its ruling class, and its outward manifestation, luxury.

There are striking commonalities between Mandeville's presentation of the workings of human vices in society and Rousseau's account of how society was founded on and corrupted by the institution of private property in a remote time when men were still near-beasts. The points of view differ, to be sure, and the points of departure as well: pride for Mandeville, property for Rousseau. Where Mandeville is all irony or paradox, Rousseau is profoundly serious. But their accounts of society in the eighteenth century coincide remarkably well. Both deal with appearances, both lift the mask of baroque society, both take in the phenomenon of luxury. And this society, as Rousseau saw and experienced intimately, was one in which "being and appearance have become two entirely different things" (*First Discourse*).

This idea had been a commonplace of baroque theater, but with Rousseau the tone was different. The distinction between being and appearance was no longer viewed as an attribute of man after the Fall, or as an object of comedy, or as part of the study of statecraft. It was perceived, rather, as an effect of luxury, and thus as an aspect of politics and society in general and of mid-eighteenth-century France in particular. Madame de Graffigny, in her highly successful novel of 1747, the *Lettres d'une Péruvienne,* noted that "the unhappiness of the nobility is born of the difficulties they find in reconciling their apparent magnificence with their real misery." But this unhappy state, in turn, was itself the result of a broader national trait: "The dominant vanity of the French is to appear opulent. Genius, the arts, perhaps even the sciences, are all related to this magnificence; everything works to the ruination of fortunes." Several decades later the Baron d'Holbach, in his *Politique naturelle* of 1773, saw luxury as having become the central passion of the whole society:

> Luxury is the situation of a society in which riches have become the principal passion. As soon as money has become the exclusive object of the greatest number of society, there can be no more powerful motive than the desire to acquire it. There is no enthusiasm but that of opulence; there is no other emulation but to procure by the swiftest of routes those signs which are admitted by all to represent power, pleasures, and felicity. (130)

From this preoccupation with money and the signs of a rich and happy life follow all the effects in society described by Madame de Graffigny, Rousseau, Helvétius, and others both before and after them in France, England, and Scotland. Unlike Mandeville, d'Holbach did not conclude that private vices in the end worked out to the advantage of society as a whole, for he saw the society itself as "infected" by that private propensity toward luxury. The critique of luxury was thus also a critique of Mandeville's paradox. Private vices may well prompt the production of luxury commodities; but to what purpose, since the rich remain bored? Indeed, perhaps it is the boredom itself which prompts art and industry to invent ever-new forms of diversion and new sensations to extricate the rich from their lethargy. Here Pascal and Mandeville agree in their critique of luxury. The ennui of the rich leads to a renewed search for and multiplication of possible pleasures; for only novelty, rarity, and the bizarre can rouse the rich from their jaded torpor. But this very intensification turns everything into a fiction. The diseased minds of the rich seek truly imaginary remedies: in Pascalian terms, divertissement cannot penetrate to the heart of the matter, the worm in the apple, the ennui in the soul.

It stands to reason, then, that the individual striving for luxury, power, pleasure, and the signs thereof does not add up to public felicity. Instead the society catches the individual's disease. The desire to possess and to display wealth reaches epidemic proportions. And yet, because of this very display, this very visibility of wealth, no one is satisfied with what he or she possesses. All become envious of one another, and no one can be happy because everyone wants to appear to be happy. There is no escape from the appearances which were the original cause of unhappiness, the unnatural, the original lie. And so everything is sacrificed to appearances; for the necessity of amusing oneself and appearing happy takes precedence over everything else. The fable of the bees has turned into the rat race.

Adam Smith had been preoccupied with the same phenomenon of the power of appearances in his *Theory of Moral Sentiments* of 1759, which can be taken as a devastating critique of appearances and an attempt to respond to

Mandeville. As a critique of appearances, it is as good an example of a critique of the Baroque as can be found. Like Rousseau and other moralists, Smith perceived the importance of appearances and the fact that men were governed by them. As much as Rousseau, he stresses the effects of the gaze of others. For Smith, to be seen is to exist; hence the pursuit of wealth:

> The rich man glories in his riches, because he feels that they naturally draw upon him the attention of the world, and that mankind are disposed to go along with him in all those agreeable emotions with which the advantages of his situation so readily inspire him. At the thought of this, his heart seems to swell and dilate itself within him, and he is fonder of his wealth, upon this account, than for all the other advantages it procures him. The poor man, on the contrary, is ashamed of his poverty. (51)

.   .   .

Now why is the poor man ashamed? In the Christian scheme of things, after all, the poor are the salt of the earth and so have nothing to be ashamed of. But Smith's analysis has nothing to do with Christianity. He too is looking for natural causes and explanations for human behavior. The poor are ashamed because poverty places the poor man, as Smith so tellingly puts it, "out of sight of mankind." To be poor is to be unseen, and therefore, in the baroque scheme of things, not to exist: "To feel that we are taken no notice of, necessarily damps the most agreeable hope, and disappoints the most ardent desire, of human nature." To be seen is to be happy. This psychology of *appearance,* or visibility, was also the very essence of court life; it was important to be seen at court, to be noticed by the king. As Louis XV put it one day, noticing the absence of one of his courtiers: So-and-so must be sulking, since I do not see him. Thus the power of appearances, and the dependence upon the gaze of others that Rousseau remarked. "The man of rank and distinction . . . is observed by all the world. Every body is eager to look at him, and to conceive, at least by sympathy, that joy and exultation with which his circumstances naturally inspire him" (51).

The life of the great and the rich thus presents images of human felicity. And men, all too inclined to take appearances for realities, are dazzled and corrupted by the exterior signs of wealth, pleasure, and happiness that are the attributes of the great of this world:

> This disposition to admire, and almost to worship, the rich and powerful, and to despise, or, at least, to neglect persons of poor and mean condition, though necessary both to establish and to maintain distinction of rank and the order of society, is, at the same time, the great and universal cause of the corruption of our moral sentiments. That wealth and greatness are often regarded with respect and admiration which are due only to wisdom and virtue; and that contempt, of which vice and folly are the only proper objects, is often most unjustly bestowed upon poverty and weakness, has been the complaint of moralists in all ages. (61–62)

In brief, men are governed through the power of imagination.

For, looked upon closely, it can readily be seen that the rich and the great govern by virtue of the flimsiest of accomplishments and talents: a certain air, a certain deportment, elegance, grace, "frivolous accomplishments," and of course rank. And Smith produces, as the supreme example of this talent for ruling by appearances, none other than Louis XIV. He ruled because he was an accomplished courtier in every respect: manner, air, walk, gracefulness, a noble and impressive bearing. "Compared with these, in his own times, and in his own presence, no other virtue, it seems, appeared to have any merit. Knowledge, industry, valour, and beneficence, trembled, were abashed and lost all dignity before them" (54). Smith makes short shrift of the accomplishments of the man of rank: "To figure at a ball is his great triumph, and to succeed in an intrigue of gallantry, his highest exploit" (55). Ultimately, in fact, these men of rank and wealth run a grave danger through their very advantages: "To those who have been accustomed to the possession, or even the hope of public admiration, all other pleasures sicken and decay" (57). In effect, they are the prisoners of luxury and of the gaze of others.

With this critique of appearances, d'Holbach, Rousseau, and Adam Smith all point to the persistence of baroque culture and a baroque mentality. In the baroque the mask was various, and played various roles: it might hide the fear of death, it might serve as a means of advancement in the world, it was a necessity at court, it might even be the mask of hypocrisy and false piety. But if we are to believe d'Holbach and Smith, in the eighteenth century the mask was that of felicity and happiness. The *douceur de vivre* which Talleyrand claimed to have existed before 1789 thus turns out to be a fiction, an illusion made possible by 1789 and its concomitant change in morality and society. The philosophes and the economists penetrated the mask and saw not *douceur de vivre* but a society sick with luxury, in which the therapeutic of divertissement had failed to dissipate the ennui in the human soul.

•   •   •

Luxury was also inextricably linked to the monarchical regime; as Montesquieu explains in the *Esprit des lois,* it is the spring or motive of monarchy. The striving after luxury is a drive for distinction. In this sense Montesquieu accepted luxury while the moralists opposed it; but he was not unaware of its drawbacks. Anticipating the later moralists and philosophes, including Adam Smith and Rousseau, he too realized that this drive for distinction, of which luxury was the outward sign, would fail to satisfy the individual.

Montesquieu's reasons for this differ somewhat from those proposed by d'Holbach and by Pascal. But they are consistent with a phenomenon described and attributed to baroque culture by the Spanish historian José Antonio Maravall, who, in his *Culture of the Baroque,* points to the growth of cities and its effect upon the individual psyche. The great capitals of the Baroque could thus, according to Maravall, become places in which individuals might already experience a "modern" feeling of alienation and insignificance. This phenomenon is also clearly linked to the aforementioned baroque desire and compulsion to be seen. This might seem a paradox, since cities are places of crowds and easy visibility; but in fact it is not. For as Montesquieu explains:

> In proportion to the populousness of towns, the inhabitants are filled with notions of vanity and actuated by an ambition of distinguishing themselves by trifles. If they are very numerous, and most of them strangers to one another, their vanity redoubles, because there are greater hopes of success. As luxury inspires hopes, each man assumes the mark of a superior condition. But by endeavoring thus at distinction, every one becomes equal, and distinction ceases; as all are desirous of respect, nobody is regarded. (Bk. 7, ch. 1)

In contemporary language, when everyone is potentially visible by means of consumer signs of distinction available to all, no one really stands out. Montesquieu is anticipating not only d'Holbach, for whom no one could be happy because everyone had to appear happy, but also de Tocqueville's views on democracy. Not only is *divertissement* a failure; luxury is equally ineffective as a means to distinction.

Yet luxury was, despite its disadvantages on the individual moral level, a necessity for the monarchical state. The monarchy stabilized luxury and put it to political use. It was necessarily linked to the social hierarchy and to unequal distribution of wealth, as Montesquieu makes clear:

> As riches, by the very constitution of monarchies, are unequally divided, there is an absolute necessity for luxury. Were the rich not to be lavish, the poor would starve. It is even necessary here, that the expenses of the opulent should be in proportion to the inequality of fortunes, and that luxury, as we have already observed, should increase in this proportion. The augmentation of private wealth is owing to its having deprived one part of the citizens of their necessary support; this must therefore be restored to them. (Bk. 7, ch. 4)

This amounts to accepting Mandeville's view of spending with no moral strictures attached, either directly or by indirect irony. Montesquieu expects the rich and the great to be profligate. From a Christian point of view this may indeed be profligacy; from a political point of view it is a necessity of monarchy. Montesquieu's views are based on an economy in which wealth is seen as a constant: what one part of society possesses, another does not. There is no question of increasing any hypothetical pie in order to increase the portions. This economic justification for luxury spending in the eighteenth century was that generally held by thinkers and others who were rather well-to-do, and while the reality was quite amoral, luxury spending nonetheless made for a moral duty: the rich had to spend so as to create work and services to be filled by the poor.

There was yet another way of looking at this unequal distribution of wealth, which was excellently put by the Chevalier des Grieux in *Manon Lescaut,* Prevost's well-known novel about an *amour-passion* that also depicts early eighteenth-century society and the relation of money to women and pleasure. The Chevalier, finding that his fortune of several thousand francs has vanished from their rented love-nest in Chaillot, knows that Manon, were she to learn of this loss, would probably be unfaithful and even leave him, since she loved pleasure and abundance too much to make sacrifices for him. The Chevalier must ponder how to rebuild his fortune—and since work is out of the question, a quick investment equally so, and borrowing is a dubious course, there remains fleecing the rich. The Chevalier's justification for this is a succinct account of what might be called Mandevillian economics:

> Most of the great and the rich are fools, which is clear to anyone who knows the world. There is an admirable justice in this; for if they had wit as well as wealth, they would be too lucky, and the rest of mankind too miserable. The qualities of body and soul are accorded these latter as a means whereby to extricate themselves from misery and poverty. Some partake of the riches of the great by ministering to their pleasures: they dupe them. Others prefer to instruct them: they try to make gentlemen of them. Only rarely, in truth, do they succeed, but that is not the purpose of divine wisdom; they always reap some fruit from their efforts, which is to live at the expense of those they would educate; and, no matter what one thinks of it, at bottom the stupidity of the rich and the great is an excellent source of revenue for the small of this world. (53–54)

Many a rogue has lived by this creed—Gil Blas, Lazarillo de Tormes, Barry Lyndon, and how many others? Diderot, in *Le Neveu de Rameau,* also supposed that the mistresses of financiers, in fleecing their lovers, were actually restituting a part of their misbegotten wealth by putting it back into circulation. At the same time Diderot looked at this world of parasites, confidence men, and entertainers of the rich with moral disdain, and with no attempt to justify luxury as Montesquieu did. Reading *Manon Lescaut* in 1734, Montesquieu thought des Grieux a rascal and Manon a strumpet. If the novel was a popular success, it was because their love was, despite their character, considered a noble passion. Yet the difference in attitude on the part of des Grieux, on the one hand, and Montesquieu and Diderot, on the other, vis-à-vis luxury and spending may well be emblematic of a signal difference between the Baroque and the Enlightenment.

Montesquieu's system supposes that one must spend according to one's rank. This is purely political and applies to the monarchical state: "Hence it is that for the preservation of a monarchical state, luxury ought continually to increase, and to grow more extensive, as it rises from the laborer to the artificer, to the merchant, to the magistrate, to the nobility, to the great officers of state, up to the very prince; otherwise the nation will be undone" (Bk. 7, ch. 4). Instead of a graduated income tax such as exists in modern progressive states, we are presented with a graduated standard of spending. Luxury, within the monarchical state, acts as a safety valve for the nobility and a means of distributing work to the other ranks of society. The nobility, stripped of real power ever since the ministries of Richelieu and Mazarin and burdened by the high cost of attendance at court since Louis XIV, could still set itself apart from the common people and make distinctions based on rank, a more or less ancient name, and a visible standard of spending. But after the firm establishment of a centralized bureaucratic state, the nobility, effectively "domesticated" into service to the king, had only one freedom left it: it remained free to spend and thus to maintain appearances. Pensions, favors, and patronage permitted the survival of an essentially baroque institution, the court, even while profound changes were slowly transforming the nation and the minds of the people.

But even this freedom to spend and to maintain the court was an illusion. For visible spending was an obligation, imposed by rank and by the necessity to keep up appearances. All of this put the nobility in the king's debt and made them all the more dependent on royal favor. Luxury thus created a society of illusion from top to bottom. Just as in the baroque world one was allowed much freedom to be creative and imaginative in the arts provided one did not question the political and social hierarchy, so in the higher social and court circles of the eighteenth century one was free to spend provided one did not question the source of the money. Spending was freedom within an absolute monarchy; it was the privilege of the great and the rich, and the aspiration of those who were not yet rich.

The political conclusions to be drawn from these reflections on luxury and its relation to the state were summed up in one of Montesquieu's most telling principles: "Republics come to an end through luxury; monarchies, through poverty" (Bk. 7, ch. 4). By 1787 the French monarchy was indeed bankrupt, but the Baroque as a mentality already belonged to the past. Luxury was still about for all to see and envy, but it was not looked at in quite the same way; and one certainly no longer reasoned about money, the great, and the rich as had the Chevalier des Grieux.

.   .   .

Of course, further distinctions involving luxury continued to be drawn and pondered. What, after all, was luxury? Mandeville, and Voltaire after him, realized that the concept was highly relative and elastic. Mandeville defined it as that which "is not immediately necessary to make man subsist as he is a living creature" (77). Luxury was thus the superfluous. But once the basic necessities of life are given, there is no limit to the superfluous, so that, as Mandeville well saw: "If once we depart from calling everything luxury that is not absolutely necessary to keep a man alive, . . . then there is no luxury at all; for if the wants of men are innumerable, then what ought to supply them has no bounds; what is called superfluous to some degree of people will be thought requisite to those of higher quality" (78). To those who argue that luxury corrupts and effeminizes society, Mandeville answers that this is not due to luxury as such but to bad administration of the state. Nor does he accept the argument that luxury enervates a state; *enervate,* to render nerveless, soft, is a word which in this case partakes of the imagination more than it sums up facts.

> "The greatest excesses of luxury are shown in buildings, furniture, equipages, and clothes. Clean linen weakens a man no more than flannel; tapestry, fine painting, or good wainscot are no more unwholesome than bare walls; and a rich couch or a gilt chariot are no more enervating than the cold floor or a country cart. The refined pleasures of men of sense are seldom injurious to their constitution, and there are many great epicures that will refuse to eat or drink more than their heads or stomachs can bear. (83)

Yet even if the exact definition of luxury could be shown to be elastic to a point which rendered the word meaningless, the phenomenon of luxury, the ever-new creation of the superfluous, could not be ignored. And while Mandeville had argued that good administration might be a guarantee against the ill effects of luxury, it is precisely these ill effects that were noted in France. Sénac de Meilhan, royal intendant and later an exile in Germany, also pondered the nature and effects of luxury in relation to the state. But whereas Mandeville had written in a period of rising prosperity stimulated by war, Sénac published his *Considérations sur les richesses et le luxe* at a time when the state was going bankrupt, in 1787. He sought to understand what was happening about him—the problem of the deficit, the visible triumph of luxury, the equally obvious indebtedness of the old nobility. As Herbert Lüthy has pointed out, the ancien régime was truly finished with the fall of Turgot and his failure to reform the system, and the consequent rise of Necker, the banker from Geneva put in charge of finances with the task of refloating the state. This signaled the end of Physiocratic economic doctrine and the triumph of a new money economy. Sénac saw this economic revolution as the triumph of the financiers, the moneyed class, over the old landed nobility. But this perspective required him to draw a new distinction, between *le luxe* and *le faste*. For after all, the monarchy and the nobility had spent lavishly on luxury. Sénac, while tacitly admitting Montesquieu's view of the intimate bond between luxury and monarchy, renamed luxury: in its function within monarchy he called it *le faste*—pomp, splendor, magnificence, grandeur.

Le faste, luxury thought of in its public capacity, lent prestige to the monarch and the state and as such was indispensable. On the other hand, the paintings, equipages, hotels, gardens, and domestics of the individual rich were "mere" luxury. A line was thus drawn between the public sector, *le faste,* and the private sector, *le luxe.* What had ruined the old nobility was its imitation of the luxury of the new financial class. The result was that described by Madame de Graffigny and the Baron d'Holbach. As the nobles grew poorer they came to be dazzled by the riches of the financier and commercial classes. The old nobility kept up appearances by conserving "a certain degree of ancient opulence which the new rich usurped in the end, but only hesitantly. The great had a considerable number of valets in brilliant livery; the rich man had but a few domestics in dull and timid liveries, but in his apartments opulence struck the eye from all parts and his table was set for the most recherché of repasts" (*Considérations sur les richesses,* 96). The nobility entered into competition with these nouveaux riches and were ruined. Sénac blames Louis XIV for this taste for luxury; he castigates the luxury of a court society based on leisure, immense inequalities of wealth, vanity, and the imitation of others. Significantly, he does not blame wealth that derives from trade or useful work, for this is a sign of national prosperity.

Sénac singles out women for particular blame in this wasteful competitition for luxury. The role of women in this world of luxury he traces to the institution of the royal mistress. The immense expenses of these women were imitated down the social scale, at court and in town, and thus woman became the arbiter of taste and thereby the regulator of expenditure: "She holds in one hand the scepter of fashion, in the other the sword of ridicule." Woman ruled through her beauty, her glitter, the veneer of fashion, the lightness of her wit, her caprice, and her love of novelty. The result was the effeminization of society: "A society in which women dominate is like a play in which they are the principle and purpose of the action. Man, in such a society, must move closer and closer to their mores and their mind. He must know how to bend to their fantasies, adopt their tastes and sentiments" (96). Effeminization for Sénac meant submission to the whims of women. The analysis of the workings of luxury thus merges with a critique of woman: baroque luxury spending had come to be seen as frivolous and feminine. It was also seen as detrimental to the arts.

2

"Doing In" the Baroque

The critique of luxury, first from a moral, later from an economic and political point of view, cannot be separated from a critique of the art of the Baroque. Critics of luxury and its effects—moralists, economists, novelists, and philosophes—were paralleled by critics of the arts; indeed, the two groups of critics often overlapped, as music, painting, and even architecture came into question. The lines of argument in the critique of the arts might seem to involve only issues of art, taste, or, to use a word not then very current, aesthetics. But taste could hardly be separated from class; to question a taste was to question those it represented. It is for this reason that the mid-century *querelle des bouffons* was far more than a dispute over opposed types of opera, French and Italian.

Opera was a court art. It was born of the court ballet, tragedy (itself a noble art form), and the pastoral, again associated with the court. Lully had made of the lyrical tragedy, as opera was also called, a royal genre: the gods and heroes of fable and history were allegorized into images of contemporary kings, princes, ladies, and courtiers. Lully's type of opera did not remain static, however, and by mid-century it had become a spectacle not only of mythology and history but also of enchantment. Opera was the world of magic, fantasy, glory, and romance, made visible through the use of machines and exempted from the demands of verisimilitude. Cervantes had laughed at the fantasies of Don Quixote, and the reader laughed with him; but neither Cervantes nor the reader would lose their sympathy for the don. The philosophes, however, much less sympathetic than Cervantes, would cast a cold eye on opera and turn a deaf ear to its music.

The quarrel of the buffoons was set off by a performance of Pergolesi's *Serva padrona* by an Italian troupe with Pietro Manelli and Anna Tonelli at the Royal Academy of Music on 1 August 1752. A war of pamphlets immediately arose. Some sixty pamphlets were produced ranging in tone and subject matter from sober aesthetic consideration to vituperative polemics. One might well argue that the Enlightenment as a philosophical movement began as much with this quarrel as with the first volume of the *Encyclopédie* and Rousseau's first discourse. Rousseau radicalized the debate over the preeminence of French or Italian music into something transcending a mere question of musical style. One may also consider the quarrel as signaling the end of the baroque world and of what Catherine Kintzler, in a brilliant study of Rameau, has called the "aesthetics of pleasure." The attack on Rameau, implicit in the debate, signified the breakup of that aesthetic. This attack on French opera was thus also an attack on the entire Rococo, for what else was a "rococo aesthetic" if not one of pleasure? The lines of demarcation between the Encyclopedists and their opponents were drawn in the course of this battle, with d'Alembert, d'Holbach, Grimm, Diderot, and Rousseau in the so-called queen's corner, and their adversaries in the king's corner and that of Madame de Pompadour: Fréron, implacable enemy of the philosophes, Cazotte, Pidansat de Mairobert, and Blainville. This *querelle des bouffons* thus also came to be known as the war of the corners—the queen's corner versus the king's corner. Henceforth the philosophes would dictate musical taste, and soon they would attempt to impose their taste in painting and architecture as well. Taste could not be divorced from politics. Indeed, taste *was* politics.

.   .   .

French opera since Lully had evolved into a genre of pure spectacle. It belonged to the category of the marvelous. Stage machinery allowed the flight and descent of gods; apotheoses were staged, as were battles, victories, and festivities; the subject matter was drawn from mythology, fable, and history. Opera united all the arts: harmonic music, melodic song, dance, poetry, painting. And insofar as it had recourse to mechanics for its machinery, and its music was calculated to produce certain effects on the audience, it was a modern genre par excellence. Its modernity also lay in the fact that it was unliterary, it was a mixed genre. It posed questions concerning the relation of language to song, words to music, dance to plot, spectacle to psychological action.

To many writers opera seemed wholly unreasonable. "Opera," wrote Voltaire,

> is a spectacle as bizarre as it is magnificent, in which eyes and ears are more satisfied than wit, where subservience to music makes the most ridiculous faults necessary, where one must sing at the destruction of a city and dance about a tomb: where one sees the Palace of Pluto and that of the Sun, gods, demons, magicians, prodigies, monsters, palaces built and destroyed in the wink of an eye. These extravagances are tolerated and even enjoyed, because at the opera one is in the land of fairies; and as long as there is spectacle, lovely dances, beautiful music, scenes of interest, one is content. (Lacombe, *Poétique de Voltaire,* 478)

Voltaire loved the theater, but it was classical tragedy and comedy he loved to act in, as it was classical tragedy he continued to write. To be sure, Voltaire had collaborated with Rameau on the *Princesse de Navarre,* a comedy-ballet composed for the marriage of the Dauphin in 1745 and later reworked by Rousseau under the title *Les Fêtes de Ramire.* And in 1745, on the occasion of the victory of Fontenoy, Voltaire also wrote the libretto for Rameau's *Le Temple de Gloire,* an opera-ballet in which Louis XV was celebrated in the guise of Trajan. But on the whole this collaboration between the great poet and the great composer was any-thing but a success, even though Voltaire recognized Rameau as a great symphonist. The contention turned on the place of poetic discourse versus that of music, just as the later dispute between Rameau and Rousseau would involve the proper role of harmony versus melody.

The issue was thus still French opera as such; the question had not yet become the more general one of art and nature and society. Indeed, the quarrel of the buffoons had been preceded by a critique of French opera which pointed out all the purely artistic or aesthetic issues later to be raised in the course of the quarrel, not to mention other, extra-musical factors. In February 1752, for example, Grimm had published a *Lettre sur "Omphale,"* an opera not by Rameau but Destouches, in which he already showed his preference for Italian music, criticizing the French use of *petits airs* mixed into the recitative as against the well-defined Italian aria. At this time Grimm still considered Rameau a great composer; when he later rejected his type of opera, it would be for reasons going beyond aesthetics to considerations of a different order.

What the philosophes liked about the *Serva padrona* was its simplicity and naturalness. As Philippe Beaussant has pointed out, however, they also liked the subject matter. In effect they were comparing incomparables, a comic opera with lyric tragedy, and criticizing the former for not being the latter. Pergolesi's *Serva padrona* and Rameau's operas belonged to entirely different categories. The philosophes liked the Italian opera because it had no gods, no mythology, no fantasy, no recourse to machines, only the simplest scenery, and a plot requiring at most four or five characters. It involved a down-to-earth, popular, comic situation easily understood by anyone, with catchy melodies that even ordinary people might sing. The music was not court music; it was not written for connoisseurs of harmony; there was no ballet to interrupt the action.

According to Beaussant, then, the attack on the music of French opera, presented in contrast to Italian opera in the pamphlets of the "war of the corners," was but a cover for a much deeper attack on Rameau's type of opera as a whole and the taste it represented and catered to. The philosophes could not take seriously an art form whose subject matter they considered pointless, a mere amusement and pleasure for the eye and ear. It was the taste of the court and the Establishment that was thus called into question. But to question precisely this art of spectacle was to question the whole baroque aesthetic and its love of illusion, play, sound, color, and dance—an art which did not pretend to anything beyond pure spectacle and pleasure.

Rameau's opera drew on his reasoned application of musical knowledge to produce illusion and thereby move the passions of the listeners and spectators. The illusion was part of the pleasure of opera: though one knew it was illusion, a game, a convention, one was willing to suspend disbelief for the duration of the spectacle. Opera was art, not life, and provided a momentary escape from life into a world of fantasy, glory, heroism, and pleasure. But it was precisely this love of illusion, of the pleasure of surprise, of enchantment, coupled with a blurring of the distinction between illusion and reality, which was essentially baroque. Life is a dream and all the world a stage. Even that tough old soldier the Maréchal de Saxe is reported to have said on his deathbed, "Life is a dream; mine has been short, but it has been beautiful." And down he stepped into his sepulcher, accompanied by France, who tried in vain to intercede with Death, who held open the casket while Hercules

mourned the great warrior: thus Pigalle's great funerary
monument to the marshal in Strasbourg (see frontispiece).
It is a splendid piece of baroque sculpture, a baroque hero's
death, and quite out of harmony with the classic deaths of
a Poussin or even a Greuze. No notary here to take down
a last will and testament, no dying father admonishing a
prodigal son, no prodigal son weeping over a dead father
wronged, no final moral; only a last act, gracefully and
majestically executed. Diderot in 1767 did not or would not
understand: "Pigalle, throw down that skeleton, and that
Hercules, however beautiful he may be, and that interced-
ing France; let the marshal lie in his last abode, and let me
see but two grenadiers sharpening their swords on his
gravestone; that is more beautiful, more simple, more en-
ergetic, and more novel than all your semihistorical, semi-
allegorical balderdash" (*Salons,* 326). The baroque opera,
the baroque imagination, had become incomprehensible to
those other minds, the philosophes. Were they not, perhaps, philistines *avant la lettre*? Indeed Diderot was calling
for a new art. But to do that was also to call for a new
society.

   At the time of the quarrel of the buffoons, Grimm wrote
that a man of wit characterized Manelli's arrival in Paris
with the opera troupe as having averted a civil war. For
public opinion at the time was dominated by the dispute
between court and *parlement*; tempers were strained, and to
some the city seemed on the verge of rebellion. Rousseau,
too, felt that his own vitriolic pamphlet against French
music had diverted attention from politics to music; Mercier later concurred. And it may well be that cultural questions merely served as a cover for political and social questions, both in music and in art criticism, for the quarrel of
the buffoons indeed went beyond opera and the question of
French and Italian tastes in music. As Beaussant points out,
harmony was the result of scholarly elaboration, of long
training, of an established musical culture; Rameau associated it with the Cartesian order. Rousseau's rejection of

harmony thus implied a rejection of this musical culture and indeed of court culture. In its place Rousseau defended what he called the music of the heart, melody. The pleasure of harmony, thought Rousseau, is that of mere sensation, and, like sensation, is short-lived and soon gives way to ennui. But the pleasures of melody were of the heart; they were the pleasures of sentiment, the passionate accents of the power of music over the soul. Rousseau opposed the accents of the heart to Rameau's scholarly structural harmony, which appealed to mind and sense. This opposition involved two aesthetic systems based on opposing concepts of nature: on the one hand, "general" nature or *la belle nature,* such as obtained in the architecture of the French garden, the "nature methodized" of Pope; on the other hand, the very different nature of the later eighteenth century, represented by Rousseau and the English landscape garden.

Kintzler associates Rameau's aesthetic with a Cartesian aesthetic based on four axioms. The truth of nature, according to the first axiom, is abstract and rests on formal relationships, presupposing an intellectualist theory of knowledge. The second axiom holds that illusion is the artifice whereby truth is revealed, which implies a sensationalist view of theatrical fiction. The third axiom has it that lyrical tragedy was devised as the double and inverse of dramatic tragedy, and is thus the principle of a theater of enchantment. The fourth axiom stipulates a constant material relation between music and articulated language, the concordance between the meaning of words and the sounds of music, and thereby the "constant co-presence of music and the spoken language" (*Jean-Philippe Rameau,* 132). All too intellectual for Rousseau, for whom music was an expression of nature. For Rameau it was an art.

·   ·   ·

Opera was not the only art form with which critics found fault; painting likewise came in for criticism. Here too much was found wanting, and here too a new breed of critic arose:

the art critic, in today's sense of the term, one who commented on exhibitions. This was novel; heretofore the discussion of painting had been left to amateurs of the arts,
members of the Academy, and scholars. These new critics
were, like the philosophes, men of letters or amateurs from
outside the establishment circles of the arts.

Dissatisfaction with the state of painting had already been
voiced in 1747 by LaFont de Saint-Yenne in his *Réflexions
sur quelques causes de l'état présent de la peinture en France*. This
little book indicated the direction that future art criticism
would take. In his criticism of the then-current modern
taste, or *petite manière,* LaFont called for a return to the grand
manner of history painting. His critique was a warning that
this art form, the grand manner, was in grave danger;
indeed, the critique itself shows that conditions had changed
to the point that his call might well be in vain. Interestingly,
the causes LaFont adduces for the decline of French painting
involved the very factors others alluded to when describing
luxury. He blamed the decline on interior decoration, the
profusion of decor we call Rococo, and the use of mirrors,
which proliferated so luxuriantly that there was no space left
for great pictures. Paintings were thus relegated to over-
doors, fire screens, and panel decorations. He also called for
the right of laymen to criticize works produced by members
of the Royal Academy of Painting, in effect admitting a new
public beyond the small circles of patrons and amateurs. At
the same time, he blamed women for the current state of the
arts, associating women with luxury (as did the economists)
and anticipating the critique of women by Sénac de Meilhan. For LaFont women were *caillettes,* gossipy, frivolous
flirts who loved knickknacks, prettiness, bright colors, the
amusing, and the decorative rather than the nobler branch
of painting, history. Madame de Pompadour had just been
received at court, and her taste would prevail for some time
to come.

LaFont's critique was suppressed by the protests of the
artists of the Academy and the establishment; but his call for
great art would not be lost on other critics, who on the

whole were to follow his lead in contrasting the grand manner of the past with the *petite manière* and frivolity of the present. Such a call for great art might be founded on two concepts: a return to the masters of the Renaissance and the Roman and Bolognese school, or a return to nature and the Antique. The first involved a reaffirmation of the baroque canon, in agreement with Horace Walpole's dictum that "all the qualities of a perfect painter never met" save in the works of Raphael, Guido Reni, and Annibale Carracci. But in a short time even this canon would be questioned as all of baroque painting came to be criticized in the name of nature, that nature which only the ancients had been close to and which only they could properly imitate.

Nature for the Baroque had been nature corrected, methodized, sublimated; it was an ideal nature, as realized in the architecture of the formal garden or the works of Poussin and Claude. By the time Diderot began to write art criticism nature had changed, and when he looked at the paintings in the exhibitions of the Salon at the Louvre he found as much wanting as had LaFont de Saint-Yenne twenty years earlier. But Diderot's orientation was more philosophical than that of LaFont, who still criticized within the canons of art, calling for a return to the grand manner but not for a new art. Diderot found fault with painting on moral, social, and aesthetic grounds. Boucher, for example, was depraved; painters catered to the taste of amateurs; instead of allowing themselves to follow nature, painters fell into a variety of manners. "There would be no manner," he wrote in his *Essais sur la peinture,* "either in drawing or color, if one scrupulously imitated nature. Manner comes from the master, the academy, the school, and even the Antique" (*Oeuvres esthétiques,* 673). To reject this was effectively to reject the long baroque tradition of imitating both nature *and* the Antique, a tradition transmitted under royal protection by the masters and the academies of painting.

But the decline of painting was also blamed on the amateurs—who, it should not be forgotten, were the great and the rich. The amateurs, those among the financier class who cultivated the arts, were seen, along with women, as a cause of the trivialization of painting and the decline of true art, indeed as an obstacle to its production. With Diderot's art criticism, the party of the philosophes was in effect calling for a new aesthetic in painting, just as it had in music at the time of the quarrel of the buffoons. If, as Beaussant has suggested, the target then was not so much music itself as court society, then with the critique of painting the target was the financiers and their taste in art: the ruling taste and the man of taste were being called into question. One could say that the dispute between the Baroque, manifest as art, and the Enlightenment, manifest as criticism, was a drama which unfolded within two critical spaces, the opera and the salons. Very different mentalities were at odds here, and on the whole the philosophes or Encyclopedists had little sympathy for the type of man belonging to the world of the arts. Diderot the philosophe did not like the Comte de Caylus, the antiquarian and amateur associated with the Academy of Painting; and Caylus did not care for Diderot. Grimm did not think much of Bachaumont, who was also an amateur. Marmontel, another philosophe, found the artists he met with at Madame Geoffrin's extravagant, ignorant, and slightly mad. Rousseau's critique of society in his *Discourses* amounted to a critique of the entire world of the arts, while the Physiocrats thundered at luxury, then an inseparable adjunct of the arts. Dupont de Nemours suggested that still-life painting might be the only truly Physiocratic genre of painting conceivable. Voltaire was different; though he had written an apology for luxury, he was hardly an amateur of the visual arts and saw no connection between art and the expression of mind. And Helvétius thought the arts were for pleasure.

In sum, amateurs might love the arts, collect with miserly enthusiasm, vainly show off their collections, and call themselves connoisseurs; but to the philosophes it was all trivia, baubles, and vanity. It was not the business of amateurs to provide direction for the arts. As Diderot wrote, painters might enjoy superiority of technique, but as regards subject matter and its representation the philosopher took precedence: "When it is a question of the ideal of his [the painter's] art, then I will have my revenge" (*Salon de 1767*, 56). The philosophes would thus tell painters what and how to paint, just as the post-Tridentine theologians had imagined and commissioned paintings to be executed by painters. The philosophical mind, like the Physiocratic, saw in the pictorial production of the late baroque world not so much what it was looking at as what it imagined: another possible pictorial universe, the sign of the philosophes' imagined world, of a reconstructed and reformed society existing in conformity with the laws of nature.

.   .   .

Diderot ponders the relation of art to luxury in his *Salon* of 1767. His reflections take the form of a dialogue with Grimm, the editor of the *Correspondance littéraire*, the journal for which Diderot wrote his art criticism. This dialogue is another of the numerous digressions within his reports on the exhibitions, digressions usually prompted by some painting or some theoretical question. In this instance it was the paintings of La Grenée which triggered the digression. Diderot found them *agréable*—pleasing—but not beautiful. The distinction is pregnant with a radical change in taste, a change which would ultimately eliminate the Rococo from the canon of good taste; it also represents a way of separating art from luxury, for the digression is concerned with the effect of luxury on the fine arts.

The assumption underlying Diderot's thinking is obvious: luxury is luxury and art is art. Diderot was not Madame de Pompadour, nor the financier who had ordered the La Grenée paintings. Luxury and works of art had, as we have seen, often been conflated, and together came under the heading of *arts d'agréments,* the "agreeable" arts. In the accounts of royal mistresses and others less royal, paintings, which to us are works of art, were often listed along with other such "agreeable" and expensive items as clothing, jewelry, bibelots, silverware, and fine furniture. On this view, similar to that of Mandeville and others, paintings were merely one manifestation of the taste of the rich and the great for possessions, pleasures, magnificence, and pretty women.

By drawing a distinction between the agreeable and the beautiful, Diderot created a means to attack baroque art on a theoretical level seemingly divorced from considerations of social class. The ruling circle and its taste could now be attacked by attacking its signs, its exterior tokens of wealth. Diderot's dialogue with Grimm is thus followed in the *Salon* by what Diderot characterized as a satire on luxury in the manner of Persius Flaccus (A.D. 34–62), whose first satire criticizes the debased literary taste of a corrupted Roman manhood and the debasement of the virtue Rome had supposedly once represented. Like Rousseau and others, Diderot uses ancient Rome as a vehicle for criticizing the art and mores of the present.

Diderot, aware that the question of the relation of luxury to the arts was a very old one, begins by rejecting the reasoning of those who had written on the question before him. As for those who looked about them in 1767 and saw the arts as being in a flourishing state, they were likely to praise luxury; those who judged the arts to be decadent, however, invariably damned luxury. Both parties, reasoned Diderot, in fact linked the arts to wealth, holding one or the other, the arts or wealth, responsible for the state of the arts according to their personal taste. A third party disliked both the arts and luxury. If the question remained confused, ill put, and unresolved, it was because all three parties based their argument on only one kind of luxury. Like Sénac de Meilhan after him, Diderot proposed to draw a subdistinction within the concept of luxury. At this point in Diderot's exposition, Grimm intervenes, telling Diderot: "Ah! you want to talk politics."

Diderot: Why not? Suppose a prince had the good sense
          to realize that everything comes from the earth
          and returns to the earth; let him then accord his
          favor to agriculture, and cease being father and
          abettor to the grand usurers.
Grimm: I hear you; let him do away with the farmers-
          general in order that he may nurture painters,
          poets, sculptors, musicians. Is that it?   (118)

To this Diderot responds in the affirmative, and proceeds
to expound a Physiocratic theory of riches: better agriculture leads to better harvests, which lead to greater riches,
which lead to greater luxury. This would seem to be merely
a restatement of the old system and all the vices of luxury
that follow therefrom. But for Diderot this luxury, based
ultimately on agriculture, is of a new type, to be distinguished from that of the farmers-general. For since one
cannot eat gold, which Diderot associates with the luxury
of the farmers-general, let the gold which they accumulate
serve instead to multiply enjoyment and

> the infinite means of being happy, poetry, painting,
> sculpture, music, mirrors, tapestries, gilding, porce-
> lain and china figurines. . . . Painters, poets, sculptors,
> musicians, and the multitude of related arts are born
> of the earth, are also the children of Ceres; and I say
> that whenever they [the arts] draw their origin from
> this sort of luxury, they will flourish and flourish
> forever. (119)

Diderot is not always as clear as might be desired, and
this is such a case. For though he may have distinguished
between two sources of art, one deriving from financiers
and one from agriculture, yet the examples he gives of the
multitude of arts born of Ceres are the same as those stem-
ming from Plutus. A truly new, uncorrupted art would
require a new society.

The Marquis de Mirabeau, the famous economist and
author of *L'Ami des hommes* (1756), was somewhat clearer

than Diderot when he considered the relation of the arts to society and luxury. Perhaps this was because he was not an artist; or perhaps it was because he, along with the other Physiocrats, had in effect "marginalized" the arts within society, in particular those arts mentioned above by Diderot. The Physiocrats, along with administrators like Sénac de Meilhan and the Marquis d'Argenson and critics of Louis XIV such as the abbé de Saint-Pierre, who thought forty million had been "wasted" on Versailles, did not regard the arts with the respect shown them by amateurs in their own time and by the various professionals of art and art history in our own time. As d'Argenson once told Voltaire: "You are but a child who loves baubles. You make more of the tassels fabricated by Mademoiselle de Chappe than of Lyons cloth or the sheets of Van Robais." Lyons represented industry, as did Van Robais, and that meant national wealth; by comparison the tassels were of minimal economic importance. Tassel makers belonged, along with others engaged in the fine arts and the luxury trades, to what Mirabeau called the world of "fantaisie"; he in fact refers to one type of worker as *ouvriers de fantaisie.* True art was not to be found in the realm of fantasy.

For the Physiocrats, the supreme art was agriculture. "Agriculture," wrote the Marquis de Mirabeau in his *Leçons économiques* of 1770, "is of all the arts the most sociable. What nobility, what generous hospitality [there is] in the mores of those who spend their lives at the head of their harvesters and their herds" (1:33). Agriculture is an innocent and useful art; it does not corrupt mores. One thinks of idyllic landscapes with happy harvesters working or resting, of grazing cattle, of still lifes of fruit and game, of images exalting the rustic life which appears as the very inverse of luxury. Voltaire linked luxury to the rise of civilization and dismissed the simplicity and frugality of the "good old days" as mere ignorance and discomfort, with no connection at all to the idealized images projected by pastoral poetry. The Physiocrats were of another mind, though they did not confuse agriculture with pastoral poetry either. Their elevation of agriculture to the supreme art implied an opposition between the natural and the artificial, between a true and useful art and the manifold products of luxury and the *ouvriers de fantaisie*. They did not distinguish between *le faste* and *le luxe* as did Sénac. Indeed, their conception of monarchy was considerably at variance with the baroque monarch of magnificence. The monarch must be at the service of the people, and not the people at his service for his glory.

The model for the arts was not only agriculture, however, but also the Antique—though not that of the Roman aesthetes, as with Winckelmann and the antiquarians. Rather, it was the practical antiquity of public works, aqueducts, city squares, public markets, roads, and amphitheaters that was felt worthy of true emulation.

As for luxury, Mirabeau perceived it much in the manner of Rousseau or d'Holbach. It was considered an abuse of riches which produced two offspring, laxity and disorder, both of which led to foolish spending. Luxury was not so much in the thing itself as in its abuse. It was also seen as a phenomenon which caused perpetual displacement and movement: nothing and no one remained in his or her place. The parvenu, for example, could thus be better off than the nobles. The social hierarchy was always being disrupted by luxury, by its visibility and that search for the visible signs of wealth and distinction already noted by Rousseau, Helvétius, and others:

> Precious furniture, magnificent dress, imposing houses, coaches and their suite of lackeys, etc., necessarily draw the gaze of the multitude, and that is what men take and always will take for distinction. In their primitive origins these things served to designate power; but when they only signify wealth, . . . luxury rules. And so emulation turns toward riches, and the emulation of the rich is only cupidity. (1:33)

Luxury is thus antithetical to honor; it also stifles the heart, leading to all the follies of fashion and foppishness. The infatuation with youth saps the structure of a society now dominated by *le colifichet* and *papillotage,* baubles and tinsel. And when youth sets the tone, the true and natural order of society is reversed, as manners, industry, and the arts are destroyed by luxury. It is not difficult to discern in this analysis of the effects of luxury another shaft aimed not only at the society of the time but also at the Rococo. The youths alluded to were not only men, but also women; after all, one wanted young mistresses.

But Mirabeau did not condemn or dismiss all the arts; he drew distinctions. There were arts which produced *aisance,* commodities, decoration, comfort, and facility: these were the mechanical arts. Then there were the liberal arts. And last, there were the fine arts. Art in its highest sense depended on a noble soul, great thoughts, and grandeur of spirit, and this alone was enough to set it in opposition to luxury. For when luxury dominates a society the arts are trivialized, and artists are forced into decadence and produce degenerate forms. In a society dominated by luxury,

> the taste for the fantastic and for novelty would spread everywhere. Noble poetry would lose its simplicity and harmony to become high-sounding and tense; eloquence would be reduced to mere witticisms, fastidiousness, and vapor; painting, *Coelum et nubes praeteriaque nihil,* would be reduced to white and pink, clouds and children; sculpture would model amors and doves; architecture become the art of building bird cages; while music, fatigued by false pastorals, would degenerate into *concetti,* tonal peculiarities, studied relations of frightening notes, concordant and marvelous to the ears of enthusiasts of the modern taste. (1:131)

And art would always have to be new, always different, always constrained to go beyond the beautiful to a point

where true beauty would be unrecognizable beneath a sur-
charge of supposedly embellishing innovation and ornamentation. Mirabeau was definitely not a partisan of the
Rococo, nor, probably of Rameau, and Rousseau might
well have been his source for this thoroughgoing attack on
the art of his time. But all this was false art; it was, in the
modern-day, pejorative sense, indeed rococo or baroque.

True art was something else. Not only was it noble and
simple, it moved the spectator, it frightened, it impressed
the thoughtful, it shook the soft. When luxury reigns, by
contrast, the pretty triumphs over beauty and agreeable
pictures over history painting. In architecture—and the period in which Mirabeau published his *Leçons économiques*
was one of splendid building—similar effects were evident.
The *hôtel particulier* is a case in point, what with its galleries,
cabinets, winter and summer apartments, vestibules, and
luxury of space, all of which confused architects and dec-
orators to the point where they no longer knew what was
wanted of them. Whereas in the past, and Mirabeau looks
nostalgically back to the manor house, the whole family
was united in organic harmony within a simple space determined by decorum, the multiplicity of spaces and decor
of the *hôtel particulier* merely served to fragment the family,
its members each going off separately to his or her own
apartment or *cabinet.* Luxury is the triumph of fantasy, and
for Mirabeau it is this which explains the present variety of
the arts and architecture, with no utility whatsoever.

There could hardly be a more consistent condemnation,
not only of luxury and its effects on art, but also of the
Rococo and the Baroque. Yet as we have seen, not all art was
condemned out of hand. Mirabeau believed in a true beauty;
even an economist could allow for art, comfort, and beauty.
Indeed, one can make the case that economics was less a
science than an aesthetic, and that the Physiocrats were a
new type of visionary.

But the relation of luxury to art, economics to aesthetics,
poses the question of consumption in the eighteenth century.

Were the Court and the Parisian
Social Elite of the Eighteenth Century
a Consumer Society?

It is tempting to read the various descriptions of the effects of luxury in the eighteenth century as symptoms of the existence of a proto-consumer society.

Rosalind Williams, in her excellent study of the rise of mass consumption in nineteenth-century France, *Dream Worlds,* thus begins with the notion of a "closed world of courtly consumption" and dubs Louis XV a "consumer king." It is true that once a year Louis XV would auction off Sèvres porcelain to his courtiers; and since Sèvres, like Vincennes, was a royal manufactory, he could by the same logic be called a royal entrepreneur. (The same could be said of Augustus of Saxony, whose veritable passion for porcelain would likewise justify the label of an entrepreneur-consumer king.) Williams also speaks of the development of "bourgeois consumption habits" over the course of the eighteenth century, presenting Voltaire and Rousseau as the representatives of opposed philosophies of consumption. The whole Enlightenment can thus be seen in terms of consumption: "The concept of *civilisation* provided an authoritative guide for the consumer—in an age when only a small fraction of the population were consumers in the sense of enjoying discretionary spending—by positing a humanistic ideal capable of giving consumption a meaning and purpose" (9).

The use of the term *consumption* here seems to equate it with civilization, since consumption was presumably subordinated to the ideal of *civilisation.* But to this reader of *Dream Worlds,* this approach seems to project our view of consumption back into the eighteenth century. For if in the eighteenth century consumption was subordinated to the ideal of *civilisation,* that consumer society was nonetheless different from ours—in which, it seems to this writer, consumption is its own end. It may well be that in the age of shopping malls, ubiquitous nonstop advertising, and the proliferation of credit cards, civilization is consumption. But it may have been otherwise in the eighteenth century. The ideal of eighteenth-century *civilisation* was far more than consumption; for Voltaire it included religious toleration and an enlightened monarchy, which meant one which did not waste wealth on wars and luxury. The elite of the eighteenth century, or rather of the Enlightenment, was not only a consumer elite but also an educated cultural elite. Moreover, the word *consumption* offers as much difficulty as the word *luxury*. One can say of consumption what Mandeville said of luxury: if everything that is superfluous and not strictly necessary for subsistence counts as luxury, then everything is luxury and the word becomes meaningless. Similarly, if everything is consumption, what does the term mean? We speak today of students as consumers, and it is not difficult to see why. But the young nobles and ladies of the eighteenth-century elite were not consuming in their colleges, academies, or convents. Williams was undoubtedly aware of the difficulties posed by the word, witness her distinction between courtly, elite, and mass consumption.

From this consumption-oriented perspective on the eighteenth century, Talleyrand's *douceur de vivre* was in effect the gentle pleasure of discretionary spending, and the history of the eighteenth century becomes that of the rich, the rakish, and the famous, with heads falling at the end. It is true that George Sand's grandmother did think life was sweeter, less gloomy, and less pretentious before the Revolution; when she looked about her in the new regime she found people glum. To this George Sand commented that the philosophy of the eighteenth century was that of the rich, wherein happiness implied an income of 600,000 livres per year. Talleyrand, and Robespierre as well, would have agreed. But does this make of the ancien régime a consumer society, or a society of a different type, in which the apparent behavior of a certain elite resembles what we now designate as consumer habits? The problem lies in the word *consumption*.

Adam Smith divided consumable goods into necessaries and luxuries. He was aware the terms were relative, and that what were luxuries in one country might be necessities in another. Leather shoes had become necessities in England but not in France, where wooden shoes were still to be found. Water was a necessity; beer and wine were not, and hence were luxuries. Classing both luxuries and necessities under the rubric of consumables, however, does not eliminate the ambiguities evident to Mandeville in the term *luxury*. Water, a necessity, can be consumed; wine, a luxury, can be consumed; shelter, a necessity, cannot be consumed. A meal in a four-star restaurant is a luxury, but it can be consumed; the tureen in which the soup is served in that same restaurant is a luxury item which cannot be consumed. An unornamented pine chest, which may be a necessity, cannot be consumed; but then an Oeben chest which serves the same purpose as the pine chest cannot be consumed either and is a luxury. One wishes economists had used better terms to describe their mental universe of producers and consumers. Left out of consideration by the economists in their distinction between necessities and luxuries is the *aesthetic* aspect of the superfluous—even in cases where the luxury truly is consumed in the strict sense of eating or drinking or wearing or destroying, as when fireworks are shot into the air, or when a beautiful city is bombarded. One thus comes up, over and over, against the problem not so much of consumption as of luxury. It therefore seems to this writer that there is an important distinction to be made between a society in a state of luxury and our present-day, consumer-service society, in which the luxury of the eighteenth century is principally to be found in museums and the problem of luxury is in large measure simply not raised.

There are certainly similarities between the Parisian and London elite of the late eighteenth century, on the one hand, and certain aspects of the life style, to use a current term, of the visibly rich and famous of today's consumer society, on the other. But there are notable differences as well. Lewis

H. Lapham, in his *Money and Class in America* (1988), quotes
from a letter of the Parisian bookseller Ruault of 1786 to
point out a parallel between the obsession with money and
the craze for speculation then and now. There were staggering deficits in both 1787 and 1987—though Louis XVI
and Marie Antoinette were considerably younger than Ron-
ald and Nancy Reagan, and memoirs on court life had to
wait until after the Revolution and received far lower pub-
lishers' advances than can be counted on in today's consumer society. The similarities are striking; they may nevertheless be superficial. It may well be that the rich of all
times behave in much the same way, or perhaps the statement is better applied only to the nouveaux riches; but they
do so under very different circumstances and in differing
mental universes. The more one thinks of similarities, the
more one also finds dissimilarities, and it may be that here
as in philosophy one is bewitched by language. We may
continue to use the word *consumption*; but the word will not
do without serious qualifications.

·   ·   ·

Herbert Lüthy, the great historian of the Protestant bank
in the France of the ancien régime, also uses the word
consumption. For him the ancien régime was an economic,
social, and political order, a hierarchical society of "inter-
connected" parts which regulated the "distribution and al-
location of functions respecting command, administration,
public order and justice." It also functioned as a system to
distribute public offices and allocate revenues—"indeed,
the ancien régime ended up being nothing else but that"
(*From Calvin to Rousseau,* 140). The upper crust of society,
the proprietors, enjoyed discretionary spending and, as
Lüthy puts it, "fulfilled with great taste, imagination, and
distinction the only social function that was left to it; namely
that of spending—while living in a lordly, noble style—the
'net product' of the agricultural kingdom" (155). The

symptoms of society in a state of luxury, as described by novelists, moralists, and philosophes, thus apply to this privileged elite, and insofar as this is the consuming class it might appear that the top of society was indeed something like a consumer society.

But the ethos behind this spending of the net product of the agricultural kingdom was not at all the same as that underlying and motivating a modern consumer society. To think of the upper strata only in terms of consumption is to ignore the crucial implications of the *interconnectedness* of everything in the ancien régime, and thereby to blur the distinction between the function of spending in the baroque society and its role in a modern consumer society. It also amounts to a blurring of the distinction between the differing functions of luxury in the two societies, and indeed between consumption and luxury *tout court*. Modern consumer societies may be possible because of the relative depreciation of what were formerly considered luxuries. One ought not to forget the function Montesquieu assigned luxury in monarchical states. Nor should one forget Mirabeau's observation that the exterior signs of wealth and magnificence no longer served adequately to signify authority—an insight revealing an awareness that *le faste* of former times and societies had indeed become *le luxe*.

Norbert Elias, in his study of court society, was very aware of the differences between a noble system of expenditure and the bourgeois view of spending. The respective attitudes of the nobility and the bourgeoisie vis-à-vis the relation of income to expenses differ radically, and the difference points out one reason for considering luxury a problem. Elias opposes a noble ethos of status consumption to a bourgeois ethos of saving for future profit. In the latter, bourgeois case, present satisfaction was sacrificed for some future gain which might be material but also social. In the case of noble spending, social position and prestige were maintained only insofar as spending corresponded to the social rank held, and not—significantly—to income. The gap between income and spending might be bridged by borrowing from a Monsieur Jourdain, or a Monsieur de Voltaire, who also lent money to nobles of his acquaintance. If this was discretionary spending, it was forced upon the spender. To cease spending according to one's rank was to lose one's *considération*. As we have seen with Adam Smith and La Bruyère before him, it was also to cease being seen, and thus to cease existing. The great in the monarchical state might have enjoyed glory, honor, and luxury, but it had to be paid for, if necessary by royal pension, and appearances were expensive—whence the rise but also the fall and disappearance, from view, of great houses.

On the level of the psychology of prestige and "visibility," that is, the need to appear opulent and happy pointed to by moralists and novelists of the eighteenth century, there is undoubtedly a parallel with today's psychology of consumption as regards the signs of distinction, affluence, pleasures, and status. But the setting and the consequences are very different. The good of the state hardly depends today on the visible splendor and luxury spending of the higher ranks of society, but rather on mass spending on consumer items, including durables which are not luxury items at all but necessities with a built-in obsolescence. Luxury had earlier been seen as posing moral, social, political, and economic problems; luxury spending today is indeed discretionary spending by a minority, but the real economic problems are posed by insufficient spending on the part of the masses. In the eighteenth century it was seriously argued that lack of luxury spending by the rich and the great would be onerous for the poor. Today the situation is reversed: the rich will not grow richer if the poor do not overspend on a vast range of so-called consumer items. A new distinction has thus emerged: the rich of the eighteenth century were not the same as the rich of today. The nature of their wealth differed, as did their economy.

Just before the Revolution the abbé Sieyès, living in a world permeated with neoclassical architecture and con-

stant references to antiquity, remarked that the world of
1788 was in reality not at all like that of antiquity. For in
fact all one heard and talked of in 1788 was manufacturing
and consumption. The older aesthetic discourse on antiquity, as we have seen, had come to be doubled by a newer
economic discourse. From our perspective, the abbé might
as well have been referring to the reign of Louis XV instead
of the ancients. For he was in fact already inhabiting a
mental world very different from that of midcentury. Luxury had presupposed not only an economy and an economics different from that of the affluent-consumer society, but also baroque display and a ruling class still relying
on or at least manipulating the outward and visible signs of
power as a means of governing, even if it no longer quite
believed in them. The critique of the Baroque consisted in
demonstrating the discrepancy between the outward trap-
pings of power, rank, and wealth, and true merit. Appearances were illusion, titles and rank a mere show. It was
Figaro's day, Figaro who reasoned like Mandeville and like
him saw beyond appearances: "Because you are a great
lord, you think you are a great genius! . . . Nobility,
fortune, rank, and position: all this makes for such pride!
What did you do for all these advantages? You took the
trouble to be born and nothing more" (*Le Mariage de Figaro*, 5.3). With that the Baroque was over, even if both the
play and the opera of *Figaro* did include a baroque mas-
querade. Society would have to be built on more than
appearances. When moralists, philosophes, and economists considered an ideal society, they now imagined one
in which merit, wealth, and power coincided with appearance. This does not mean that these formed the basis of a
consumer society such as our own, but rather of a society
of production, free trade, and a balanced budget. This was
seen as coinciding with the natural. Consumption would
no longer be decided by rank, but by the market. And
riches would no longer be luxury.

•   •   •

And yet it is undeniable that even if eighteenth-century London and Paris society was still not quite a consumer society as we understand and experience it—that is, involving consumption based on mass sales and continuous advertising campaigns, gift shops in museums, mail-order catalogues, and so forth—nonetheless the critique of baroque appearances and court spending, coupled with the eventual destruction of baroque society in France during the Revolution, loosed forces that would eventually make possible the type of consumer society we are acquainted with today. But first the triumphant bourgeoisie of the nineteenth century would have to imitate the life-style of the old court and town nobility; only then could the image of the sweetness of life pursued by the old court society come to be marketable in the form of tourism, palatial hotels, furniture styles imitating those of the past, eclectic millionaire architecture, and the dream world of romanticism.

The Enlightenment, considered as an anti-Baroque, made possible an economics emphasizing rational productivity and capital accumulation coupled with productive investment, rather than the luxury, glory, and deficit spending of the Baroque. Such an economics does not make for a consumer society, but for one geared to productivity. But concomitant with this call for economic liberalism came the invocation of nature and liberty, the attack on the prejudices of the past, the secularization of society and the consequent secularization of the Pelagian heresy, to wit, the idea that man was not irremediably damned—all coinciding with a call for the liberation of sensibility. An unwitting product of economic liberalism was thus the romantic sensibility. Madame de Staël wrote a novel demonstrating that love might triumph even over poverty; Monsieur Necker, her father and a banker, countered with one demonstrating that it could not. Jane Austen was very much aware of the same question. Romanticism, like economic liberalism, was based on dissatisfaction. In the words of Jacques Bousquet, "Romanticism and economic liberalism are equally founded on dissatisfaction; instead of seeking inner contentment in the present situation, one must always ask for more, at any price and in all domains, whether in sentiments, impressions, or consumer goods" (*Le XVIIIe Siècle romantique,* 126). Romantic individualism and aspirations and economic individualism thus have a common source.

Over the course of the eighteenth century, money triumphed over the barriers set against it by Christianity, feudal values, and secular moralists like La Bruyère. Some of the old nobility, like Madame de Beaufort in Madame d'Epinay's novelized memoirs, might still maintain that "bread and honor, my child, are all one needs to live"; but fewer and fewer agreed with her. The new nobility, the financier class, the aristocracy of money in the making—all held a different view, as did Monsieur d'Epinay, who led a life of dissipation. Significantly, the word *dissipation* had both an economic and a moral meaning, and the two were inextricably linked. When Madame d'Epinay went out to the theater or the opera it was called dissipation by her elders; when Monsieur d'Epinay spent a small fortune on his mistresses it was not only moral dissipation but also indiscreet spending and, worse, the incurring of debts. By the end of the eighteenth century, the force of opinion was overwhelmingly against the beliefs of a Madame de Beaufort. But was the age for all that a consumer society?

It was certainly the age of the triumph of money, and the power of money undermined traditional structures, values, and beliefs. The rich, in the beginning of the century, had not been looked upon favorably. As the moralist Le Maître de Claville put it in an oft-reprinted work:

A too-lively attachment to wealth is of all the passions the most shameful, the most tyrannical, and the most harmful to the one possessed by it; it is the most dishonorable vice and the one which leads to the greatest injustices. It marks at once a character both base and inhumane; it leads to one's own suffering and the suffering of others, deprives us of pleasure and enjoyment, delivers us up to trouble, agitation, disquiet; in a word, it has almost all the traits of infamous avarice. (*Traité du vrai mérite de l'homme* 2:78)

But moralists notwithstanding, wealth was a reality, it made itself visible through luxury, and the increasing wealth of individuals and society at large was a reality which merited pondering. If for Monsieur d'Epinay it meant the pleasures of dissipation, for Madame d'Epinay it meant certain responsibilities: "It seems that all is said in the world when one enjoys a hundred thousand livres' income and a name. And I say that wealth is good only for making us accountable to the public for our tastes, our opinions, and that it further deprives us of the right to complain and the sad consolation of being pitied" (*Histoire de Madame de Montbrillant,* 209). In a sense one might argue that eighteenth-century society was not so much a consumer society as one pervaded by the temptation to dissipation and baroque spending, a temptation countered by a new type of moralist: the economist, who would teach the age how to spend properly, wisely, and morally. The economist's point of view was essentially bourgeois, and this was incompatible with the baroque mentality. What this means, however, is that baroque dissipation is closer to modern consumerism than is the economic thinking of the eighteenth-century economists.

In a brilliant novel, *L'Ecole du sud* (1991), Dominique Fernandez explores the difference between baroque Sicily and France and comes up with illuminating insights into the difference between baroque society as manifest in southern countries like Italy, Spain, and Austria—in short, Catholic nations—and Protestant countries such as Holland, England, Scotland, and northern Germany. This north-south dichotomy involves religious attitudes which influence spending. Thus Catholicism is a religion of expense, as witness the magnificence of Roman churches; Protestantism is a religion of restraint, of unornamented, sober, aus-

tere churches. The differences made for strong states in the
north and weak ones in the south. France occupied a mid-
point between north and south and managed to create a
strong state in spite of Catholicism because its Catholicism
was Jansenist, or Augustinian, in its theological orientation.
Its morality, for practical purposes, was almost Protestant.
What happens on the secular level of the arts in eighteenth-
century France is parallel to this religious Jansenism: baroque and rococo art, manifestations of the southern spirit
of costly magnificence and expense, come to be opposed by
the austere style of the Antique and a morality of bourgeois
productivity.

Redesigning the Ancien Régime

In accounts of the French Enlightenment, a central role is
usually assigned to the philosophes—Montesquieu, Voltaire, Rousseau, Diderot, and the Encyclopedists—and to
materialist philosophers like Helvétius, d'Holbach, Condillac, and La Mettrie. These are the "party of humanity,"
to use the happy expression of the historian Peter Gay.
Think of the French Enlightenment, and the philosophes
come to mind; think of the European Enlightenment as a
whole, and these figures are joined by the philosophers
Hume and Kant, as well as the so-called enlightened despots
like Frederick II, Catherine the Great, and Joseph II. Think
of the economics of the Enlightenment, and the Scots with
Adam Smith at their head come immediately to mind; the
Physiocrats or French economists may perhaps be mentioned in passing.

Yet despite the above-mentioned emphasis on philosophy, by 1789, and certainly thereafter, the world answered
more to the elucubrations of the economists, whether
French or Scottish, than to the ideas propounded by the
philosophes or philosophers. Where Voltaire negated,
where Montesquieu defined ideal types in history, where
Diderot speculated and Rousseau dreamed of an ideal re-

public, the Physiocrats redesigned society, so that by 1788 the abbé Sieyès could write in *Qu'est-ce que le Tiers Etat?* that "political systems, today, are founded exclusively on work; the productive faculties of man are everything" (7). There is no question here of the glory of arms, the prestige of kings, ancient lineage, or tradition. It seems a far cry from the pleasures of the Rococo, the *douceur de vivre* of Talleyrand, the wit of Voltaire, or Rousseau's ideal republic and his exaltation of nature. Sieyès presents students of the French Enlightenment, or of the history of art during that period, with a far different Enlightenment, that of manufacturing and consumption, not salons, drawing rooms, and the life of the court and the battles of literary and musical critics. There is thus a very literary Enlightenment centered on the philosophes and the writers and artists, and another founded on an alternative literature, that of the economists and the would-be reformers of the social system. We say "founded on an alternative literature" because the new world described by Sieyès, which was also that of Adam Smith, was really an alternative *aesthetic* system vis-à-vis the baroque aesthetic. Given the system of the economists, a grand design, presumably the work of a divine order, had somehow gone wrong over the course of history because of a Fall—not that of Adam, but a Fall nonetheless. Man had now to set himself to work to somehow recover God's original intention, an intention which coincided with that of nature. For it was agreed by many that man had not been irretrievably corrupted by the Fall, and that a Christian life need not always be an austere, puritanical one of self-denial and deprivation. Economics, when it first attained to theoretical autonomy, could be construed as a means for letting God's invisible hand do its work of restoring the lost Garden of Eden.

If in Scotland and in the Kingdom of Naples and the Two Sicilies economists were to be found in the universities, in France they were to be found in Parisian salons, at court, and in the provinces. By the end of the reign of Louis XV, the French economists had already been designated as a sect; Adam Smith noted them as having a great following; they were talked about, published books, invented a new vocabulary, and ran a journal, *Les Ephémérides du citoyen*. This last word is worth noting: citizen, not subject of a king, but member of a state. Though partly in disagreement with their doctrine, Smith saw their importance and wrote in *The Wealth of Nations* that their "system . . . with all its imperfections, is, perhaps, the nearest approximation to the truth that has yet been published upon the subject of political economy, and is upon that account well worth the consideration of every man who wishes to examine with attention the principles of that very important science" (642). Their economics, however, implied a change of the social order and fiscal reform; thus their man in government, Turgot, fell even as Smith was publishing his famous treatise in 1776.

Yet they had had their man at court, Dr. Quesnay, founder of the sect, physician to Madame de Pompadour, and author of the famous *Tableau économique*. They had a doctrine; they had a system; they had answers or remedies to the present ills of society; and they expounded their system with the aid of a new vocabulary or jargon and through the *Tableau économique,* which graphically represented by means of mathematical formulas and intersecting lines the distribution of wealth in an ideal economy of perfect liberty and high productivity. Their economic model implied more than a better economy; it implied a better society.

The *Tableau* was rather difficult to decipher; like the grand paintings representing scenes from ancient history which were soon to appear in the yearly exhibitions of the Academy, the economic tableau too needed written explanations for the uninitiated. The economists, however, also had a slogan, one which *was* easily understood and is still very much alive today: *laissez faire, laissez passer*—let the economy alone and nature will do the rest. While Adam

Smith referred to economics as a science, it was hardly a pure science; for these early economists were also visionaries, and their science sometimes appears more like an aesthetic vision. The economists had a vision of the natural order and man's place in it, as they had a vision of the future city of man within that natural order—an order they divined by looking to a remote past, though one less remote than that of Rousseau. They were at one with Rousseau on the corrupt, unnatural state of contemporary society.

Jurists and apologists for the status quo tended to describe eighteenth-century French society as a God-given order comprising the traditional three orders of society: clergy, nobility, and third estate or commoners. When the Estates-General were called in 1789, the delegates were classed according to this traditional system. The reality, however, was different, and in many of the writings of the time the social structure was described not in terms of the three orders but by more complex gradations corresponding to wealth and to function within the state. Thus Jean Domat, in his *Droit public* of 1697, classed ranks on the basis of dignity, authority, necessity, and utility into nine levels: clergy; profession of arms; counselors of the prince; administrators of justice; professionals of finance, sciences, and liberal arts; commerce; industry; artisans; and agriculture and animal husbandry. Things had become even more complicated by 1770, when Louis Sébastien Mercier drew up the following classification for the population of Paris: princes and great lords; lawyers and jurists; financiers, from farmers-general to money changers and money lenders; dealers and merchants; artists; artisans and workers; lackeys and the lower people. Restif de la Bretonne, in his *Contemporaines par gradation,* 1783–85, established a hierarchy of women ranging from duchesses to women of the stage, a total of twelve categories; with further subdivisions, including women of the streets, he arrived at thirty-seven grades.

There was general agreement on certain broad principles of social ranking: the sword had more prestige than the law, which took precedence over finance; after these came men of letters, then the *négociants* or traders, and finally the lower orders of society. But conflicts of precedence rendered the task of classification more complicated. The nobility of the sword, for example, was not one homogeneous bloc; while the court nobility may have been well-to-do, the majority of the nobility were less well off, and many were even poor. Yet all were nobles with, as Montesquieu put it in his *Lettres persanes* of 1721, ancestors, a sword, and debts. All this was changed by the Revolution; and even before that event, the Physiocrats had laid out a program for the theoretical re-organization of society.

The economists started with a clean slate by eliminating rank, privileges, precedence, prestige, and tradition, and substituting the notion of class. They retained the sacred number three, dividing society into three classes: propri-etors, producers, and the sterile or unproductive class. This was considered a natural order, since in the Physiocrat view all wealth actually derived from the cultivation of the earth, from nature, and the classes were defined by their relation to the ownership of land, that is, to the cultivation, nurturing, and furthering of the fertility of nature. Though a natural order, it was nonetheless instituted by God—not the same God as that of the Christians, to be sure, the economists not being theologians, but nonetheless God. The standard of classification expounded by the Physio-crats—no longer based on feudal or Christian precedent, or on tradition or the idea that the nobility belonged to some superior race, but on property and one's economic role within the order of nature—thus implied not only a redesigned society but also a redefinition of human des-tiny.

No wonder, then, that the economists were called a *sect*. Like a religious community, they had a catechism of thirty articles, all beginning with the imperative "Que" ("Let"), with the overall title "Maximes générales du gouvernement agricole le plus avantageux au genre humain." The first five articles read:

I.   Let the sovereign Authority be One and superior to all individuals in Society and all unjust enterprises of particular interests.

II.   Let the Nation be instructed in the General Laws of the natural order which self-evidently constitute the most perfect government; for the Nation, through its knowledge of these laws, must concur with the Sovereign to establish the best of all possible laws.

III.   Let the Sovereign and the Nation never lose sight of the fact that it is agriculture which multiplies wealth.

IV.   Let real estate and personal property be assured to their legitimate owners; *for security of property is the essential foundation of the social order and of the improvement of the land* [emphasis added].

V.   Let taxes not be destructive of or disproportional to the gross income of the Nation; let tax increases follow increased revenue; let taxes be directly based on the net product of the estate.

And so on for twenty-five more articles of economic faith, articles which in effect also amounted to a statement of general principles of government. Jeffersonian minimal government followed logically from these precepts.

The economists were stupendous simplifiers. Their system of thought rested on a new trinity, natural rather than supernatural: God, Nature, and Property. The whole Christian-baroque drama of fall and redemption, the tragic view of life and the providential view of history, the established baroque ideas of glory, honor, play, noble gestures, tragic failure, and comic relief, the concepts of sacrifice and martyrdom and sainthood—all these were swept aside as attention turned to nature and man's physical needs. The God of the Physiocrats was not the Christian God, but could be that of the Deists, Socinians, or latitudinarians, or that of the Dutch traders and Swiss and Genoese bankers,

or even the God of Newton, artificer of a universe which
ran in an orderly, regular fashion according to immutable
natural laws.

This grand order also implied a new morality. Within the
order of nature the three classes all had a role to play, just
as in the former society the three ranks had had a role to
play. But the roles of the new natural order were no longer
sanctioned by the supernatural, and consequently good and
evil were, so to speak, dethelogized and naturalized. Like
modern politicians, the Physiocrats promised a better and
happier world, so long as one followed the maxims of the
great order of nature. What did God ask of mankind? Sacrifices? Martyrdom? Withdrawal from the world to a life of
prayer and meditation, or a life of repentance for original
sin? God, explained the Marquis de Mirabeau, only expects
man to fulfill himself within the system He had instituted.
Man must use his intelligence and his faculties to attain all
possible happiness. Let man be wise and just, and realize the
full enjoyment of his being. Let his desires, successes,
hopes, and fears be lived within that great bosom of Providence whence he received his life and being, to which he
must refer all his endeavors, and to which he will one day
return. The system of the economists was nothing if not a
natural religion with distant echoes of stoicism.

For the Physiocrats, education consisted in teaching the
natural laws which governed the great order, of which
individuals, like the monads in Leibniz's grand design, were
integral parts. The essence of all instruction, no matter what
one's role in society, was thus *economic*: to learn the rights
and duties of man according to nature and to cultivate the
economic use of one's intelligence, for the purpose of as-
suring one's subsistence and satisfying one's needs and desires. It was not enough, for example, for a pastry cook to
suppose it in his interest to sell as much pastry as possible.
He must also understand the whole chain of interests
whereby the pastry cook and the pastry he made were
linked to the farmer who grew the wheat, the miller who

ground that wheat into flour, and the merchant who bought
the flour and sold it to the pastry cook. The order of nature
was thus conceived as a linkage of private interests which,
if left free, added up magnificently to public happiness and
public wealth.

Voltaire's satire notwithstanding, all was for the best in
the best of all possible economic orders and worlds. Optimism as metaphysics might have been laughed at, doubts
might arise as to the existence of monads, and the notion of
the necessary relation between cause and effect might be
called into question; but optimism appeared to survive *in* if
not *as* economics. The vision of a happy and wealthy society
of free individuals, each pursuing his own interests on the
basis of a true, natural economic order, was something akin
to the mystical vision in the baroque religious sphere.
Christian charity was out; *bienfaisance* was in. Saints were
out, and monks dismissed as parasites; happy, wise, pru-
dent, and responsible landlords were in, coexisting with
grateful laborers in idyllic landscape and village settings, a
harmonious union of proprietors and producers.

Society was formed of naturally free individuals who
must all know and understand the natural order on which
their happiness was founded. They must all work together
for a happiness which rested on one sacred and inviolable
right: the assured possession of property, and of those pre-
rogatives and attributes of property necessary to the prosperity and fruitfulness of all classes in society. The relation
of the individual to society thus rested on property, the
exploitation of that property, and especially the proper
circulation of money.

The problem with money in the eighteenth century, the
Physiocrats felt, was that too many thought money to have
value in and of itself. Money as gold and silver was shiny,
beautiful, palpable, hoardable, and transformable into
plate—all of which tended to keep it out of circulation. A
true Physiocratic society precludes Molière's miser. In the
natural order of things the miser is more than ridiculous: he

is almost criminal, since his failure to invest his funds threatens the proper circulation of money. On the other hand, Balzac's old man Grandet, who knows just when to sell his wine for maximum profit, is eminently a member of Physiocratic society. For the Physiocrats money is merely an exchange commodity, a token of the true riches which come from the soil. Too many proprietors, unfortunately, confused money with riches. Forgetting the common interest existing between those who own the soil and those who work it, they tried to get as much money as possible from their produce, thereby creating tensions between producers and proprietors. Social conflict thus did not arise from unequal distribution of property, but from the false wealth of money; this, not true riches, made some men oppress others. Money was there to be used, and used wisely, as water was used to fertilize soil. For money fertilized investment, and as such could be regarded, in Mirabeau's words, as the "thermometer of the order of labor and expenses" (*L'Ami des hommes*, 1:83). But money was not an end in itself. Here the Physiocrats could agree wholeheartedly with all those who condemned the ill effects of luxury on society.

As noted above, the natural order also implied a moral order. Man had natural rights, which were admirably balanced by natural moral duties; the right to subsistence was balanced by the duty to work. The property owner may not have had to work in the sense of tilling his land himself; his duty, rather, was proper investment and management. The man of leisure was thus an anomaly in this system, and to do nothing could be regarded as a kind of crime. The sins of human nature in the supernatural order became social crimes in the natural order, and guilt survived along with natural inequalities and social inequalities. There was thus no place for the spendthrifts, scribblers, musicians, courtiers, artists, adventurers, gamblers, spectators, lovers of luxury, amateurs, connoisseurs, *curieux,* monks, nuns, and priests who had featured so richly in baroque culture. The nephew of the famous Rameau, immortalized by Diderot, was a parasite such as could only have been found, and could only have survived, in a corrupt and denatured society. It was thus not at all illogical that the Physiocrats also considered luxury a problem, and that, as we have seen, their system implied an art different from that of the Baroque.

·   ·   ·

Just as the triumph of Madame de Pompadour at court signaled the triumph of the financier class over a more traditional court nobility, so the social triumph of Monsieur Necker (thanks to his wife), coupled with his later elevation to supervisor of the royal finances, signified the defeat of the Physiocratic party in government circles and a return to traditional measures for dealing with the ever-growing problem of the deficit. From the standpoint of Physiocracy it might appear as the triumph of the sterile class. Scribblers sang the praises of Monsieur Necker; his wife proclaimed him a genius; he had written an essay in defense of Colbert, therefore he was a writer, therefore a philosophe, therefore the man to resolve the problem of the deficit. Necker's eulogy of Colbert, published as part of the controversy over free trade, had favored state intervention in that dispute and thus taken a stand against the Physiocrats. In this he showed himself a friend of the people, always afraid of bread shortages and high prices, and therefore also of free trade.

But this early piece from Necker's productive pen was insignificant compared to what he accomplished once in charge of finances. For Monsieur Necker did something absolutely unheard-of: he published his budget report to the king, his famous *Compte rendu au Roy* of 1781, and made of it an international best-seller. The famous phrenologist Lavater, feeling Monsieur Necker's cranial bumps, recognized genius. In the eyes of Sénac de Meilhan and other critics, on the other hand, he was seen as a manipulator of funds—another borrower and, as such, part of the problem rather than the solution. Necker, like the philosophes, also lifted the mask of the Baroque, though in a different way: he showed how expensive it was to maintain a court. According to the royal accounts made public in January of 1781, the king's domestic household, including buildings and grounds, cost 25,700,000 livres; pensions for the courtiers were even higher, 28,000,000; while the funds allocated to the crown prince and his spouse and the Count and Countess d'Artois amounted to 8,040,000 livres. Only the cost of the war against England in alliance with America exceeded these expenses, coming to 65,200,000 livres—not counting the ordinary war funds, artillery funds, and navy funds before the war, which were also high, 31,000,000 livres. By comparison, foreign affairs cost a relatively low 8,525,000 livres, and the maintenance of royal roads and bridges only 5,000,000. These revelations hardly endeared Monsieur Necker to pension recipients. But with this bestseller of a budget, made public against custom, Necker was opposing what he considered a modern, efficient government to baroque expedients. Economics and the Baroque were antithetical.

In exposing the court as wasteful, in pointing out that the government machinery needed reform, Necker was in accord with the Physiocrats. But he differed from them regarding their assessment of the so-called sterile class, and in the vision of society which might be construed from his writings. For example, where the Physiocrats had posited three classes in society, the banker from Geneva saw only the rich and the poor, that is, property owners and those without property. It was a view also shared by the abbé Sieyès, who similarly posited, in effect, two peoples within one nation: "A great nation is necessarily composed of *two peoples,* the producers and the human instruments of production, the people of intelligence and the workers who have but a passive force, the educated citizens and the auxiliaries to whom is left neither the time nor the means to receive an education" (*Qu'est-ce que le Tiers Etat?,* 10). And in Necker's view of the natural order of things, the rich would get richer and the poor would get poorer over the course of time. For the differences between the two were too great and too many to be overcome—even assuming they ought to be overcome, which at the time no one really supposed. After all, the differences between rich and poor were natural, due to natural inequalities. To be sure, a wise administrator might have certain obligations toward the poor, such as keeping bread prices down so that the poor might not go hungry in times of poor harvests. But this was not charity but a matter of policy: the poor must be assured subsistence in order to go on producing and working for the rich. On a sentimental level, charity was replaced by *bienfaisance* and the paternalism of the rich. Madame Necker, like Madame de Pompadour, founded a hospital. *Noblesse oblige*: nobility imposes obligations, and so do riches.

Another distinction between Necker and the Physiocrats lay in the frankness with which he drew the line separating rich from poor. No question here of the common interests of proprietors and producers. Necker did not hold to the view that the exchange of subsistence wages for working the land of the proprietors was "fair" in that so much labor could be equated with a certain amount of money. Rather, he used the word "exploit" to characterize this transaction, and all the profit in the exchange was on the side of the property owners. The exchange was as unequal as the poor were different from the rich.

It is curious to note how the hallmarks of superiority of the baroque world, the awe inspired by the great and the noble, are by Necker attributed to the rich. The poor, by contrast, are not merely another people in the same nation; they are like different beings. Quantitative difference is thus turned into qualitative difference. The poor live from day to day, they are dressed in rags, they inhabit hovels, they live in hunger and sickness, and they have no part at all in culture. Indeed, they ought not to be educated: "In a state of unequal fortunes, the result of the social order, instruc-

tion is forbidden to all men without property" (quoted in
Grange, *Les Idées de Necker,* 117). The result is that the poor
have an infantile, almost primitive mentality; swayed by
superstition, imagination, and emotion, they are naturally
religious. Religion satisfies their craving for the irrational,
and especially so a religion which presents them with images, charms the eye, and is filled with pomp, ceremony, and
the representation of mysteries. For these reasons the poor
can hardly be trusted with the management of affairs. They
do not have the capacity for sustained reflection; they must
be led by the hand, and for the stability of society they must
remain passive, preoccupied with bread for their bodies and
religion for their souls. Needless to say, they have no refined feelings; marriage for them is merely the putting
together of two single miseries, because misery can be
better tolerated together than alone.

Fortunately for society, the mentality of the poor is such
that they naturally accept the rich and the splendid as creatures of a different order. But if the poor were capable of
thought and could rise to the level of abstract concepts, the
result would be very dangerous indeed. For then they might
begin to reflect (as did Rousseau) on the origins of society,
property, and social rank, and would see these as contrary
to their interests. Inequality of knowledge is thus just as
necessary as the other inequalities in society.

Necker is in effect defining the new elite of the late
eighteenth century, and, though of course he does not use
Marx's words, he sees religion as the opium of the people.
The rich had culture; the poor had superstition and the
consolations of the life to come. Necker himself was not
particularly a man of culture; but his wife and daughter
more than made up for it, a pattern that would recur in the
later bourgeois culture of the nineteenth century. This separation of cultured women from money-making men may
well have been an effect of the end of the Baroque and court
society. In any event, the culture and luxury of the world
were all for the rich, and signified the new elite of the rich,

the propertied, the educated, the well-mannered, and the refined.

It follows that Necker also differed from the Physiocrats on luxury, though not radically. For him, as for most thinkers by the end of the eighteenth century, the one negative aspect of luxury was prodigality, now associated not only with the spendthrifts of Mandeville but with princely splendor. Otherwise luxury followed logically from both social and economic inequality. It was the necessary and natural result of the naturally unequal distribution of property. Equal distribution of property would be a disaster; for individuals would then work only to satisfy their needs, a crucial spur to agricultural production would thereby disappear. Fortunately, property was unequally distributed, and great landowners would always exploit their land beyond their needs, not only to pay labor costs but also and primarily to satisfy their desires. As with Mandeville, egotism, desires, appetites, and love of luxury are seen as the motive force behind the whole economy, so that luxury is a positive development and the effect of a flourishing economy, not the result of the poverty of the many and wealth of the few. Both poverty and luxury exist because of the unequal distribution of property; since this is natural and normal, luxury is as normal as poverty. Thus luxury is not the symptom of a diseased society requiring a different diet, as a doctor like Quesnay might have put it, but, to the contrary, of a modern, civilized society.

Only prodigality counts as a pathology, symptomatic not so much of disease as of a *dérèglement des moeurs,* to use Necker's term. The grand seigneur who goes bankrupt, as we saw with Montesquieu, is implicit in the very system of honors and dignity presupposed by the monarchy. But for Necker that grand seigneur is harmful to the state. Baroque spending—the *grand geste,* the *bella figura*—is beyond Necker's essentially bourgeois mind. If he distinguishes between two types of luxury, it is not politically, like Sénac, but on totally different grounds. There is luxury due to

inequality of property, which is normal; and there is prodigality, which is due to personal failing or "unruly mores."
To teach his son to spend liberally, the duc de Richelieu
emptied a purse out the window into the street. This gesture
would have been incomprehensible to Necker. He indeed
does not understand baroque spending: "The luxury most
inimical to political economy is that which is contrary to the
increase of population. Such is the luxury of parks, magnificent roads, and horses, because it uses for magnificence
and amusement a great portion of land which could otherwise have been capable of increasing subsistence" (quoted
in Grange, 110). Ruin for the nobility was in the baroque
order of things; balancing the budget and spending within
one's means was in the bourgeois order of things. With
Necker in power, the Baroque expired in the red.

The abbé Morellet, reflecting in his memoirs on the
causes and the essence of the French Revolution, felt that
Necker did not understand either economics or the true
notion of property. His views on Necker and property are
an excellent summary of the new society implied by the
economists:

He [Necker] had failed to understand the rights of
property as concerns trade for the products of agriculture and industry; nor did he understand any better
the rights that property has in government, which, in
the last analysis, is nothing other than the protector of
property. He did not see that once one ceases to regard
the government as a fact, and wishes to reorganize it
according to rules and found it upon law, it can only
be founded on the right to landed property; that
henceforth only property owners have the right to
establish and institute government. It was thus no
longer as nobles or as priests or as members of the
Third Estate that deputies might form the Estates-
General, a constituent assembly, but as property owners and in virtue of landed property, whether hered-
itary or usufructuary, sufficient in itself to be a
guarantee of their real interest in public affairs, of the

requisite instruction to handle them successfully, and
of the leisure to engage in such work. (*Mémoires,* I:145)

Failing to take these truths about property into account
when the Estates-General were called, the reform of the
government eventually turned into a revolution of the poor
against the rich. For the representatives elected to the Es-
tates had been chosen to represent the three Orders of the
realm—clergy, nobility, and third estate—and not all such
representatives were landowners. Morellet and other economists, however, assumed that the right to elect representatives and to act in the government ought to be restricted
to property owners. Thus in 1793, at the moment of the
Terror and the regulation of the price of bread, the city of
man envisaged by the economists—based on property and
social hierarchy, from poor to rich, from the nonpropertied
to men of property, and equated with the natural order of
things—was seen as under attack, and the Revolution itself
was taken as an attack on the sacred rights of property and
the natural order.

The Earthly City of the
Eighteenth-Century Philosophes

We opened our examination and exploration of baroque
spending and its implications by pointing to the palace and
the formal garden. We might equally well have begun with
the baroque city and its grand squares, avenues, and urban
palaces and gardens and fountains, all of which were also
signs of royal magnificence. But the baroque city was also
a place of great contrast, of luxury and misery coexisting
side by side. In 1771 Louis Sébastien Mercier published a
vision of a reformed Paris which, though it did not abolish
the baroque city, yet offered the image of a city which could
be interpreted as that of the economists and philosophes, an
image of what a successful Enlightenment might have pro-

duced. As the Physiocrats envisaged a natural order of work
and virtue, so did Mercier dream of a Paris of work, virtue,
enlightenment, and natural simplicity. In Mercier's Paris, as
in Ledoux's ideal future city, the Physiocrats' assumptions
as to a natural order based on the fertility of agriculture were
reconciled with the Enlightenment respect for science and
the liberal economists' acceptance of trade and commerce as
productive forces.

Mercier's vision of the future took the form of a novel
entitled *L'An 2440, ou rêve s'il en fut jamais.* The narrator of
this tale or dream, born in Paris, like Mercier himself, in
1740, oversleeps seven hundred years and awakens to find
himself still in the city of his birth. But the year is now 2440,
and Paris is an improved and reformed city in which vice,
luxury, poverty, and misery are no longer to be seen. This
ideal Paris contrasts with the real Paris—both before the
Revolution, as Mercier describes it in his twelve-volume
Tableau de Paris, which appeared from 1782 through 1788,
and after, as in his *Nouveau Paris,* published in 1800. In the
real Paris the rich are set against the poor, luxury is jux-
taposed with the utmost misery, and the city is plagued with
pollution, noise, bad taste, and overcrowding, the result of
sacrificing the provinces to a city that has become a mon-
ster.

In Mercier's dream Paris, some of the plans under discussion in Mercier's own time have at last come to fruition.
The Louvre has been connected to the Tuileries, statues
occupy the niches of the Pont Neuf, houses have been
cleared from the Pont-aux-Changes (a demolition depicted
by the painter Hubert Robert), the Bastille has been torn
down, though not because of a revolution, and a Temple to
Clemency has been erected on its site. Bouchardon's equestrian statue of Louis XV is still in its place and still much
admired. Mercier thus finds himself in a renewed Paris,
clean, airy, and spacious, supplied with ample water and
graced with elegant fountains. The old steep Gothic roofs
have disappeared, and houses are now topped with roof
gardens.

As for Versailles, it lies in ruins, abandoned. The monarch resides in Paris, the capital of a flourishing state in which luxury is unknown and religion itself has become rational. Mercier visits the Temple of God, a rotunda with a magnificent glass dome supported by a single row of columns and entered through four great portals. The altar to the God of Reason is set in the center of the Temple, illuminated by the natural light of heaven penetrating through the top of the dome. The Temple has neither statues, allegorical figures, nor pictures of saints or martyrs. Religion has been purified of all superstition and the accretions of the ages. As such it is the very inverse of baroque religion, just as the Temple is the very inverse of the baroque church with its painted ceilings, representations of saints, candles, incense, chapels dedicated to the cult of saints, and dramatic altarpieces. Mercier's Temple is the Pantheon, now the home of a primal cult presented as a natural and rational religion.

This new, natural, rational religion is, ironically, the result of economy. Mercier's account of his Temple to the Deity should be read in conjunction with Diderot's article "Pain béni" (Communion bread) in the *Encyclopédie*. In that article Diderot argues against the use of bread in Communion, and the argument is entirely economic. He calculates that there are in the realm some 40,000 parishes in which such bread is distributed during Mass, sometimes twice a day, not counting confraternities. At forty sous (two livres) apiece, this comes to an expense of 80,000 livres; multiplying that by 52 Sundays yields the staggering sum of 4,000,000 livres per year. Think what four million livres a year could do for charity! Furthermore, the consecrated bread is no more sacred than the water used to bless it, so that water would suffice for Communion instead of wine. The same calculation is then applied to the candles used during Mass and generally burnt for religious purposes in church. This is dismissed as vain decor; any reasonable person would agree that three-fourths of the candles so used could easily be saved. Given about 80,000 churches in France, Diderot figures that each church could save fifty livres per year; multiplying by 80,000 churches yields a savings of four million livres. The argument is worthy of the United States Congress discussing poor relief. It is also an irrefutable indication of the passing of the baroque mentality.

Pondering Mercier's dream Paris, one begins to see that, though expanded in space, it is a Paris reduced and diminished in life and spirit, a kind of Calvinist Geneva on the Seine. Remove from a city what the disciples of Rousseau and the economists called vice and luxury, and the city and its society become what the abbé Du Bos justly termed *le séjour de l'ennui,* the home of boredom. All is reduced to virtue, and the past and its riches, its religion, and its comforts have been eliminated. But then the Paris of 2440 presumably enjoyed full employment.

But vice and luxury are not the only things done away with in this Cartesian sweeping away of the errors of the past. Literature too has been almost entirely eliminated. As religion is reduced to *bienfaisance,* or good works, so literature is reduced to morality. When Mercier's narrator visits the Bibliothèque Royale, he finds the reading room has decreased to a very small space, and the 200,000 volumes and 70,000 manuscripts to a few hundred volumes, if that. The errors of the past have been burned away. What has been thought worthy remains, but abridged, expurgated, and amended in keeping with the true principles of morals. Homer, Sophocles, Euripides, Demosthenes, Plato, Plutarch, Herodotus, Sappho, Anacreon, and Aristophanes have been burned. Virgil, Pliny, Titus Livius, and Sallust survive, but Lucretius is reduced to extracts, as is Cicero. Ovid and Horace are expurgated, Seneca reduced to a fourth of his oeuvre; Tacitus can be read only with special permission, Catullus and Petronius have disappeared, Quintillian is reduced to one thin volume. English literature, on the other hand, shows the largest number of volumes on the remaining shelves, where one can see Milton, Shakespeare, Pope, Young, and Richardson. Italian literature is represented by the *Gerusalemme liberata* and Beccaria's treatise on crime and punishment. French letters are as reduced as the Latin. All of Jean-Jacques Rousseau, however, survives, as too Montesquieu's *Esprit des lois,* the *Bélisaire* of Marmontel, the famous *Telemachus* of Fénelon, and Helvétius's scandalous work, *De l'esprit,* while the *Encyclopédie* has been re-edited on a better plan. Corneille, Racine, and Molière survive, along with La Fontaine, la Motte, J. B. Rousseau, and certain works of the eighteenth-century polemical lawyer Linguet—but also, and very significantly, Mirabeau's *L'Ami des hommes,* one of the literary monuments of Physiocracy. All too obviously, the antiquarian element inseparable from a library has been eliminated, along with the love of books and the love of reading. After all, according to Rousseau, in a virtuous society literature is superfluous, for virtuous citizens have no need of divertissement.

It is illuminating to contrast Mercier's future Royal Library with another fictional library of the eighteenth century, that of the great senator Pococurante of Voltaire's *Candide.* Pococurante is rich, but he is also bored. He is bored with the courtesans of Venice; he is beginning to be bored with the two lovely maids who serve Martin and Candide chocolate on their call to the senator; he is bored with his paintings, including his two Raphaels; and he easily becomes bored with that most baroque of art forms, the opera.

After an excellent dinner Candide and Martin are shown the library, where Candide spots a splendidly bound Homer which, he thinks, would be the delight of his old tutor Pangloss. But Homer holds no delight for Pococurante. He explains that once he was persuaded to believe that he found pleasure in reading Homer, but no more; indeed, all the sincere people he questions admit that the book falls out of their hands. But one must have him in one's library as a monument from antiquity, just as antiquarians must have rusty medals in their cabinets. But what of Virgil, asks Candide? The second, fourth, and sixth books of the *Aeneid* are good enough, but the remainder are cold and boring; Pococurante prefers Tasso and the tales of Ariosto. And Horace, queries Candide? There are useful maxims to be found there, but as Pococurante explains: "Fools admire everything in a celebrated author. I only read to please myself, and I only like what suits me" (309).

Candide is impressed by such fastidious taste; Martin finds that Pococurante is simply *dis*-gusted. Pococurante is still a man of the Baroque: he reads for pleasure, he judges on the basis of pleasure, and so he may still be placed under the general baroque rubric which Catherine Kintzler has aptly referred to as the aesthetics of pleasure. But Pococurante's world is a world in transition, coming just before the end of the Baroque; for it is obvious that divertissement is failing, that men can have too much taste, too many pleasures, and that ennui will have to be overcome by means other than the divertissement of the arts.

With Mercier we are beyond the aesthetics of pleasure, in an enlightened world where the arts have been subjected to moral judgment. Pococurante may have been bored; he may not have touched most of his books; but he did not burn them. His library is still of the Baroque, full, splendid, rich, and the delight of those who, like Candide, have not been spoiled by wealth and pleasures. The contrast between Mercier's future library and that of Pococurante is the contrast between the Enlightenment with its utilitarian principles and the Baroque.

In the future Paris of 2440, it is not only the Royal Library which has changed. The French Academy, like the Royal Library, has also survived into the distant future, though transplanted to Montmartre and housed in another of the temples to be seen in the new Paris. The members of the new Academy are now housed in small rustic dwellings placed about the temple. The reason for these individual dwellings are obvious: genius, thought, and reflection were associated with solitude, withdrawal into self, quiet, and friendship, rather than with the worldly endeavors, flattery, and intrigues of eighteenth-century literary Paris. As for the Cabinet du Roi, it too is transformed, into a vast Temple of Science formed of four immense wings and surmounted by the greatest dome ever seen. Mercier's description of this Temple of Science is reminiscent of one of Boullée's designs for his huge Metropolitan Church.

The Academy of Painting has also been reformed along moral-utilitarian lines, indeed along lines which might well have pleased art critics of the Diderotian persuasion as well as those who had urged a program for the production of history paintings that might depict, in visual form, the progress of history from the Dark Ages to the more enlightened ages. Significantly, the picture representing the eighteenth century is a figure of a woman bedecked with jewels and trailing her luxurious dress in the mud—a mixture of rags and riches, and as such an allusion to the illusion of luxury. The picture, as Diderot might have said, is "hieroglyphic," and patently a sign.

Amateurs, *curieux,* collectors, connoisseurs, antiquarians—these figures of the art world of baroque culture have of course no place in the Paris of 2440. In a sense, the new city takes no account of the sterile class simply because it has none. The city has become one vast moral, productive, economic-scientific center justified by and based on the natural order of things: "There is not a day man must remain unoccupied or useless: like nature, which never abandons its functions, man must reproach himself for leaving his. Rest is not idleness, inactivity is damage to the Fatherland, and the cessation of labor is in the end a diminutive form of death" (*L'An 2440,* 1:111). Obviously unemployment has been eliminated along with luxury. Mercier's dream city is a very busy but also very virtuous hive, and his city comes as a latter-day answer to Mandeville's paradoxes.

The role of women, too, has changed considerably from what it had been in the baroque culture. There is no talk of royal mistresses, and in a city without luxury women are neither creatures of nor consumers of luxury. Rather, they have been turned into virtuous mothers, the consoling companions of men—yet subordinate to men, as is only natural. Consequently they are virtuous, honest, loving, sweet, modest, caring, and patient. Their accomplishments are no longer dancing and music; on the contrary, women study economics, the art of pleasing their husbands, and raising children. Clearly these women have been nurtured on the economic catechism rather than on licentious or frivolous novels. Their education precludes both Madame de Pompadour and Madame Bovary.

One may further surmise that this virtuous city precludes characters such as that grand baroque parasite, Rameau's nephew. Nor does one imagine Casanova in this dream Paris—though one can envision Diderot there, perhaps teaching a course on public morality, or economics as morality. For Mercier's dream Paris involves not only new monuments, but also a new morality of which the monuments are the signs.

•   •   •

Mercier's vision of the Paris of the future may seem to be that of a materialist; the survival of Helvétius's *De l'esprit* in the Royal Library is not insignificant. On the other hand, the preservation of all the works of Rousseau in the same collection points in another direction, as does also Mercier's account of the Temple of the Deity. This temple is not baroque, nor does its God emerge from any baroque vision, though He might have satisfied baroque metaphysicians. The Temple is erected rather to glorify Newton's God, the architect of the universe and its regular motions. Yet the sacred was not banished from this ideal city of Mercier and the philosophes, for the Temple was a direct link to a remote past in which architecture had been connected with the sacred, with a forgotten language of signs, and with a primitive, natural, rational cult common to all mankind—a natural religion linked to agriculture, and far less abstract than that of the philosophers or metaphysicians. Dissatisfaction with the established, de-natured order of society led some critics to envision a reformed society based on a model which they found in a very distant past, a time they called the "primitive past," just after the state of nature envisaged by Rousseau but before the Tower of Babel. This primitive past was that of a lost agricultural state. Such considerations point to a link joining Mercier's vision of a future Paris with similar intellectual currents of the time: with the elucubrations of architects inspired by that same distant past, with the grand speculations and researches of Antoine Court de Gébelin on a lost primitive universal language, and, through him, with Physiocracy.

As art critics found fault with the painting of the Baroque, so there also arose critics of architecture who found the modern style an aberration from the original laws of that art. While the abbé Laugier in his *Essai sur l'architecture* of 1753 posited the origin of architecture in the primitive hut and took as an example of pure architecture the Maison carrée at Nîmes, Jean-Louis Viel de Saint-Maux traced the origin of architecture to the sacred and to agricultural cults in his *Lettres sur l'architecture des anciens,* published from 1779 on and issued in a one-volume edition in 1787. In these letters he unraveled the symbolic meaning of architecture and its basic elements, such as the column, the capital, and the pediment. Architecture was linked to the sacred, to agriculture, to a lost language of symbols. This theory shifted the discussion of architecture away from such issues as relative versus absolute beauty, the emphasis on the orders, or the anti-luxury polemic launched by the abbé Laugier, and toward the function of architecture within the city and its relation to religion and nature.

Viel de Saint-Maux's interpretation of ancient architecture was based not only on accounts of monuments as given
by travelers, ancient texts, and archaeology, but also on the
work of Court de Gébelin, author of the nine-volume *Monde
primitif.* Court de Gébelin fleshed out the abstractions of
economic theory with a concrete historical and linguistic
justification of these theories. It is as if *Le Monde primitif*
were, so to speak, the Bible vis-à-vis the catechism of the
economists. He presented the vision and even the recon-
struction of a lost primitive society in which language,
mankind, and nature were one harmonious unity.

Court's system was succinctly described and analyzed by
the abbé Joseph-Marie Le Gros in his *Analyse des ouvrages de
Jean-Jacques Rousseau et de Court de Gébelin* (1784), a most
revealing work. The juxtaposition of Rousseau and Court
de Gébelin is not fortuitous: both were Protestants, both
were obsessed by the idea of the Fall, and both gave this idea
a new interpretation, a *historical* meaning. For Rousseau,
man fell from the state of nature, his version of the state of
grace, into society and history; for Court, man fell from a
grand natural order of primal unity into the present disorder.

According to Le Gros, Court's system rested on one
fundamental assumption concerning human destiny: that
"obedience to the great order is the sole road to perfection
and happiness, and that disobedience is the inevitable road
to depravity, ignorance, and misery" (126). Though instituted by God, this great order was materialistic, for it rested
on man's *physical* needs, necessity, the resources of a re-
gion, and the proper road to happiness within that order.
This insistence on human needs links Court's system to
Quesnay's *Essai physique sur l'économie animale* of 1736, one
of the founding texts of Physiocracy; in neither scheme was
there any questions of saving souls, as was assumed in
Christianity. There were three parts to Court's argument:
the primitive world was good and happy because men
obeyed the laws of the great order and were in harmony

with nature; the modern world is unhappy because it disobeys this great order; and the modern world is ready once more to take the road to happiness by again accepting the laws of this great natural order.

For Court de Gébelin, man was distinguished from other animals in his use of words, *la parole,* and in his use of agriculture. He was endowed with certain natural rights, in particular that of self-preservation, a right complemented by his first duty, to provide for his subsistence. His second duty derived from the first: to render agriculture as productive as possible, for a productive agriculture made possible the Physiocratic *net product,* which was the fundamental principle of economic science and the source of all prosperity. Agriculture was thus the foundation of all human activities, and religion itself in its original pristine state was agricultural. Contributing to the increase of the net product was thus fulfilling one's religious duty on earth. This original religion recognized a Supreme Being that had in the remote past been honored under the guise of the moon, the sun, the stars, and such elements as fire and water. Festivals were instituted to thank the Supreme Being for the bounty provided by nature. Prayers were directed to the Deity to bless the work performed over the seasons; religious holidays were thus grounded in plowing, sowing, and harvesting, with days of rest breaking up the labor of the year. Agriculture was not only the first art, it was also a difficult art, and accordingly had to be glorified and made more agreeable through festivals and various seasonal ceremonies. In these ancient festivals lie the beginnings of music, dance, and poetry.

The origins of society were thus marked by unity: one language, one system of writing, one grammar, one religion, one cult, one government, one code of laws, one ethic. "The government," explained Le Gros, "was naturally composed of a single sovereign, a paterfamilias, fulfilling the functions of counselors, great property owners, cultivators, and salaried employees. In this type of agricul-

tural government, founded on nature, the sovereign gave
no orders, because all the rights and duties were prescribed
by Nature herself" (142). This ancient and natural system
or order, a species of theocracy without priests, also implied
an iconography. The ancient gods of the Greeks and Romans were assimilated to this original agricultural cult:
Saturn was the inventor of agriculture, Mercury the inventor of the calendar and of astronomy, Hercules presided
over the clearing of forests and the dredging of swamps, the
Dioscorides were linked to commerce and navigation,
Poseidon to fishing, Diana to hunting, and Bacchus to
the grape harvest. The gods of fable had become the gods
of agriculture. The gods who served the modern painter
as mere decoration were in fact the signs of this ancient
religion, whose forgotten meaning was the key to the
mentality of the primitive world, just as its surviving monuments with their inscriptions and signs served to recon-
stitute the original language of mankind.

The modern world is the result of the loss of this natural,
primitive great order and unity. The Fall was not a myth,
but a series of historical events which occurred about 800
B.C. and may be attributed to the Chaldeans and the conquests of Nebuchadnezzar. These invasions and conquests
were detrimental to the net product, and ushered in a long
period of warfare in which the ancient order of the arts, the
sciences, and even writing, that "primitive art invented in
the very beginning and thus necessary to agricultural societies to maintain their prosperity" (142), was lost. The
results of this fall and the ensuing period of strife were still
evident in the eighteenth century, in which wars were
fought with money rather than men, genius was stifled, and
men feared thought and innovation. Modern cities were
another sign of this distant fall; they were sources of corruption and the tangible evidence of modern man's decadence.

The idea of linking agriculture to the sacred and rein-
terpreting mythology in terms of an ancient agricultural

cult was not new. Both the abbé Pluche in his *Histoire du ciel* (1741) and Corneille de Pauw in his *Recherches philosophiques sur les Egyptiens et les Chinois* (1753) had pointed in the same direction. But both had posited a priestly class as keepers of the mysteries. In Court's system such a priestly class was not necessary, since the laws of the great order were known to all by way of nature. But there is something to be said for seeing the economists themselves as a kind of substitute priestly class which has rediscovered the ancient and natural order. Given that writing is necessary to an agricultural state, one can think of the economists as the scribes keeping accounts of the net product from season to season. The Physiocrats were not referred to as a sect gratuitously. They acted rather like a new priestly class— revealing the mysteries of economics with the help of a new vocabulary, bringing the word, showing the way to a happy society through increased net product and a system of distribution made visible by a sign, the *Tableau économique* of Quesnay. It remained only for some architect to actually create a new Jerusalem, in which nature and the city might work in harmony as part of the great order of nature.

·   ·   ·

The moral utiliarianism of Mercier, the emphasis on the sacred origins of architecture and its link to nature, and various assumptions of the Physiocrats were all to be echoed in the plans of Claude Nicolas Ledoux's ideal city.

Ledoux's *L'Architecture considérée sous le rapport de l'art, des moeurs, et de la législation* (1802), takes us beyond the Enlightenment of Voltaire, skepticism, reason, science, and common sense. But Ledoux's vision does not necessarily go beyond the Enlightenment of the Physiocrats and other dreamers and visionaries who conceived of an improved, reformed mankind and society, indeed perhaps a recovered great order. We are not suggesting that Ledoux read Court de Gébelin and then proceeded to draw up the plans for an ideal city which might reflect that great order. But Ledoux must have elaborated his plans during the French Revolution, which was, among other things, an attempt to reform not only the state but society and mankind itself, so that to understand it, as Tocqueville rightly saw, one must think in terms of a religious phenomenon.

As an architect Ledoux was admirably suited to design such an ideal city. He had a great deal of experience behind him in both the private and the public spheres. Not only had he designed houses for Madame du Barry, and the Hôtel Thélusson for a rich Genevan banking family, but also the great customs wall around Paris, which was to make the collecting of customs for the Ferme Générale more efficient even as the city of Paris was made more beautiful; and he had even designed what may be called a factory town complete with working and living quarters, the salt works at Arc et Senans in the Jura foothills. He was also thoroughly versed in the theory and practice of the more baroque *architecture parlante,* or expressive architecture.

His friend the abbé Delille, the indefatigable versifier, tells us in his poem *L'Imagination,* written between 1785 and 1794, that Ledoux's ideal city was to be dedicated to Plato, the creator of an ideal Republic. This link to Plato is enough to make one doubt the validity of associating Ledoux with the Enlightenment, and certainly with the Enlightenment of a Voltaire or even a Rousseau. Yet there is one aspect of this city which does link it to the Enlightenment of the Physiocrats: the dream that in the ideal city mankind would find happiness. In Delille's words:

> There would happiness be and there the human race
> Admire the most beautiful phenomenon:
> Modest dwellings and superb palaces,
> Flowing fountains and clear rivulets,
> The counters of Plutus, the father of fortune,
> The forge of Vulcan and the workshop of Neptune,
> The temple of Themis and the arsenal of Mars,
> The storehouse of knowledge and the studio of art,
> The circus of combat and the pomp of the stage,
> Where Thalia smiles and Melpomene weeps;

All in that vast city's breast
Pleasure and necessity command,
All that may fecundate human industry,
Adorn, enrich, enlighten, and the fatherland defend.

Where Ampion had but built the fabulous walls of Thebes,
Ledoux would build a world.

  This world of Ledoux's, despite Delille's classical allusions and the supposed dedication to Plato, was very much
of the eighteenth century, and founded on end-of-century
realities. His ideal city may be read as a synthesis of the
moral, economic, and aesthetic assumptions held by the
economists and the philosophes of the late Enlightenment.
The contradictions of baroque culture—reality and appearance, misery and luxury, vice and virtue, art and nature—
are resolved and reconciled in this ideal city, and agriculture
and commerce work in harmony therein. Ledoux's city
may have been a utopian vision, but it was founded on the
realities of capital, industry, labor, and the sacredness of
property, and on the life, liberty, and happiness promised
by the great order. And it was a liberty inseparable from the
order of virtue—or the circle of the good, as Ledoux himself
put it—since the architecture itself, through its forms, beauties, and charms, would induce the dwellers and workers of
the city to be virtuous. As Ledoux wrote: "One may be
virtuous or polished, as a pebble is rough or polished, by
the rubbing of what surrounds us" (3). Architectural
forms, surfaces, and effects of light and dark would affect
the psyche by acting on the senses, so that the city would
in effect be linked to the universal principles of attraction
and repulsion.

  Ledoux seems here to combine the sensationalism of
Condillac, assimilated to architecture by Le Camus de
Mézières in his *Génie de l'architecture* of 1782, with the Newtonian notion of cosmic attraction. In effect, the classical
ideas of the beauties and harmonies of proportion are supported by the scientific laws of universal attraction, an

attraction determining not only the courses of celestial bodies but also of human beings. Ledoux's architecture is thus linked to the cosmos and its universal laws. He speaks of abundant harvests, full breasts, and grateful vegetation, of labor stimulating the resources of nature to production and fertility. His images are not only those of architecture and the Newtonian cosmos, but also reminiscent of an agricultural tableau, of men at work in harmony with nature. Buildings attract or repel by their effects on the soul; men and women are attracted by desire; commerce itself is seen as a form of attraction. Ledoux's universe is one of circulation; one may think of the mesmeric fluids which circulate throughout the cosmos. It partakes of the great order of things, in which the principles of nature are communicated directly to man with no intervention from a priestly class.

Architecture can also speak directly to man by acting directly upon the eye of man, thus in effect functioning like the natural signs which the abbé Du Bos had distinguished from the artificial signs of writing. True architecture is a primary language, a sign system more effective than abstract signs and reasoned precepts: "Give us models which speak to the eye; they will make a greater impression than precepts, than that multiplicity of writings which weigh upon thought only to confound it" (Ledoux, 52). The *architecture parlante* of the Baroque thereby turns into an *architecture écriture*. Ledoux's buildings in his ideal city are signs that signify their function in the cosmic order—from the regularity and solidity of the stock exchange, which regulates the flow of commerce, to the phallic design of his Oikema, which reforms vice by the principle of repulsion (the sight of vice will impel to virtue), to the central location of the director's house in his salt works, the various public buildings dedicated to harmony and justice, and the communal and even individual buildings designed around the functions of their inhabitants within the city and the great order underlying it.

In 1791 the Comte de Volney, another late eighteenth-century philosophe, produced *Les Ruines, ou méditations sur les révolutions des empires*. In this well-known work a traveler to the ruins of Palmyra is surprised by the Spirit of the Ruins, lifted by that spirit over the world, shown the rise and fall of empires, and told the lesson of history. This turns out to be the lesson of the Physiocrats and Court de Gébelin: empires fall when they cease to obey the laws of nature, which are simple and clear—liberty, equality, justice. Ledoux conjured up a city which would never fall precisely because it was built on natural laws. This city, like the world of the Physiocrats, knew neither luxury nor idlers. Yet it was not without taste; for the recovered great order could not have failed to entail the recovery of true taste as well.

3

True Taste Recovered and
the Baroque Transfigured

When Saint-Preux, in Rousseau's famous novel *La Nouvelle Héloïse,* steps into Julie's garden, which she calls her Elysée, he finds it is as if he has not stepped into a garden at all, but is rather the first to set foot on some distant isle far from civilization. He seems to find himself in what the eighteenth century often referred to as a "desert," which meant not some Saharan waste but verdant nature far removed from the intervention of man. Paradoxically, one may say that Saint-Preux found himself in natural nature. The enchanted isle of Ariosto, which Louis XIV had imitated in a series of festivals to inaugurate Versailles and its gardens, had turned into the island of Robinson Crusoe. Indeed Emile, the subject of Rousseau's experiment in education, had read Defoe's famous book as part of his moral and practical education, which was devised to preserve in him a natural virtue in a corrupt society and to make him free and independent, a kind of natural man in a non-natural society. Julie's version of nature thus had the appearance of pure nature, a nature which the Baroque had rejected as imperfect and not worthy of imitation, preferring instead to construct an ideal nature, an emanation of reason, a nature corrected. If in the Baroque the grotto of Thetis might dazzle the eye and astonish the soul, by the end of the

eighteenth century there was greater charm to be had from
the simple joys of nature. Formal gardens were art; hence
they were artificial luxury, and as such were coming to seem
as boring as other aspects of baroque luxury. And they were
in bad taste, they were ostentatious; as Monsieur de Wolmar, Julie's husband, puts it:

> I see in these vast and richly ornate grounds only the
> vanity of their owner and of the artist; the one is ever
> driven to show off his wealth, the other his talent, and
> both at great expense prepare boredom for those who
> are supposed to enjoy their work. A false taste for a
> grandeur that was never devised for man always ends
> up by poisoning his pleasure. A grand air is always
> sad; it evokes the miseries of those who assume it. In
> the midst of one's parterres and *allées,* one's own little
> individuality can hardly expand, and a twenty-foot
> tree would cover one as well as a sixty-foot tree; the
> body takes up only three square feet and can become
> lost in a sea of possessions like a mite. (360)

Rousseau's point of view is utterly at variance with that
of Mandeville or with the observations of Adam Smith,
who noted the expansive nature of the rich and the increase
of the self through riches and possessions. But then Rousseau was hardly at ease in the Parisian salons of the great and
the wealthy, and from his unease with baroque grandeur
and splendor, he constructed an aesthetic experience at variance with that of the Baroque. A man who would not enjoy
himself in a garden such as Julie's could only be a person of
unhealthy taste and unhealthy soul. Rousseau has eliminated *luxe d'ostentation;* in its place he has introduced *luxe de
mollesse.*

·   ·   ·

In *Emile* (1762), his treatise on education, Rousseau distinguished between two types of luxury. One was familiar

to critics of luxury; the Marquis de Mirabeau had used the term in his economic writings. This was *luxe d'ostentation,* luxury *tout court* for Sénac de Meilhan, associated with the financier class and the power of money in society, and also called prodigality by Mandeville and Necker. This luxury of ostentation was external glitter, visible show, and unmistakably baroque. But Rousseau also wrote of *luxe de mollesse*—a rather novel concept, and quite unlike ostentatious luxury or what Veblen was later to call conspicuous consumption. *Luxe de mollesse* was internal, and referred to a state of the soul. It was the enjoyment of the simple things of life and of nature herself, such as Rousseau must have experienced in his rowboat as he dreamed and drifted on the lake of Bienne at a moment of his life when he found a few weeks of peace on the Ile de Saint-Pierre. According to this celebrated passage of his *Rêveries,* Rousseau felt at one with the universe. He had what we may call an aesthetic experience connected not with some work of art but with the cosmos. Rousseau can also be said to have found himself at one with that great order of nature later to be described by Court de Gébelin, with one telling exception: Rousseau was not being productive in that great order, he was dreaming. But the significance of the experience was indeed a feeling of unity with nature; *luxe de mollesse* was the natural luxury of *dolce far niente,* the joy of simply existing.

Ostentatious luxury was associated with the rich; but this does not imply that *luxe de mollesse* should be associated with the poor, for they have no time to enjoy their existence and the simple things of life and nature. Rather, *luxe de mollesse* may be associated with a new kind of man of taste, corresponding to Rousseau's interpretation of the English gentleman and man of taste as depicted in another character from the *Nouvelle Héloïse,* Sir Edward Bomston. Sir Edward speaks of the fine arts with discernment but without pretension; he judges of their quality by feeling rather than by rules; he has been to Italy and, being a man of feeling as well as taste, he loves Italian music. Sir Edward Bomston is Rousseau's response to his own *First Discourse,* in which had begun his general critique of baroque society and its arts and masks. He manages to inhabit a corrupt society without himself being corrupted by it, and his love of Italian music places him beyond the baroque standard of taste and within a new aesthetic.

•   •   •

Whereas luxury could not, in the final analysis, satisfy the desires of the rich forever or quiet the anxieties of those who suffered from ennui, taste might just do that. Since Pascal and Du Bos, the arts had been considered as a kind of therapeutic of ennui. Even Rousseau accepted this principle, acknowledging that in a corrupt society the arts might be of some use. With mankind too far gone to recover a lost innocence, plays and novels had become necessary in a negative way: better to read about vice than indulge in it.

But the Pascalian and Dubosian aesthetic of divertisse-ment, and indeed this whole aesthetic of pleasure, came to be seriously challenged, in all its aspects. The *querelle des bouffons* questioned the aesthetics of Rameau's opera, which is that of pleasure expressed through harmony; Diderot questioned the conventions of theatrical representation, of baroque painting and sculpture, and, in his praise of Rich-ardson, of the novel as then established. Rousseau's *Nou-velle Héloïse* was an example of the new taste or aesthetic, as were the new types of gardens in the Anglo-Chinese manner, gardens presumably closer to nature than formal gardens. The failure of baroque aesthetics, the aesthetics of divertissement and pleasure, was the moment of birth of what later came to be known as the "aesthetic experience," which was in fact nothing but a profane version of the mystical experience of the baroque saints. Rousseau had a mystical experience of nature, Winckelmann in Rome had a mystical experience of beauty as manifest in works of ancient statuary. This implies a shift of attention away from a work of art as a work subject to conventions, rules, the judgment of taste, to the *experience* of a man or woman contemplating a work of art or a work of nature. Thus taste as a standard of judgment gave way to the experience of the work, and romanticism was at hand. In the words of a Jane Austen title, sensibility triumphed over sense. In terms of aesthetic theory, the end of the baroque aesthetic meant that a work of art had now to be founded on "the natural."

A case in point is the Comte de Saléran, a fictional character from the novel of the great architect and teacher Jacques-François Blondel, *L'Homme du monde éclairé par les arts* (1774). The Comte de Saléran, like the rich described by Helvétius and d'Holbach, was bored. The count had tasted of all the luxuries and all the pleasures that life and wealth could give him. Had he been born a hundred years later, he would have been described as decadent; not so in 1774, however, with the aesthetic era only just begun. A friend suggested that he interest himself in the arts, and there he found his salvation from ennui. His spirit, as he put it, was raised to the brilliant sphere of the arts; he was transported to a sojourn of enchantment; he saw the light; he found a new source of voluptuous pleasures; the heart he had exhausted, the senses he had lost, were restored by this interest in the arts, and he found himself like a man reborn. The baroque vision and representation of divine ravishment, indeed its very language, have here been transferred to the contemplation of the arts and of beauty. But Saléran's journey away from the pleasures of the world of wealth implies that this new interest in the arts is something different from luxury, from the possession of works of art, from mere pleasure. The conversion of the Comte de Saléran to a love of the arts implies the separation of ostentatious luxury from art. The task of taste was to effect this separation on the theoretical level. And this operation, the separation of art from luxury, was to have major consequences. For the new aesthetic, this new enthusiasm, implied at the time the dismissal of most of the art we now call baroque in the name of true taste. What the Count acquired was precisely *taste,* judgment in the arts, the capacity to reflect upon his new-found pleasures.

．　　　．　　　．

By 1770 the man of taste was hardly a new figure, though he had usually appeared in the narrower role of amateur, connoisseur, *curieux,* dilettante, or antiquarian. As such, however, he had not always been a figure worthy of admiration. La Bruyère in his *Caractères* considered the type under the heading of fashion, whereas he dealt with literature and writing under the heading of works of mind or wit. Curiosity was dismissed as a passion: "Curiosity is not a taste for what is good or what is beautiful, but for what is rare, unique, for what we have and others do not. It is not an attachment to what is perfect but to what is sought after, to what is in fashion" (406). As for amateurs, Diderot and the other philosophes disliked them intensely. Yet critics of both French opera and the pictures displayed at the salons appealed to taste when making their judgments. The man of taste, then, was by the 1760s clearly something more than an amateur, connoisseur, or *curieux*.

Father Bouhours and Boileau under Louis XIV, and Dryden, Pope, and Shaftesbury in England, had all, in the wake of Gracián and Bellori, been writers and poets who taught the art of discernment in literature and pictures. By the same token, they were also the ones to establish taste, by providing examples of works which were thought to constitute good taste. The battle pitting judgment by taste against judgment by rules had been fought and won by taste. Pedants might write of the rules of art and poetry, but the public judged by sentiment. The man of taste thus exercised what Du Bos had called the *goût de comparaison* within his area of predilection, be it poetry, painting, architecture, sculpture, or music. His judgment was based on sentiment, and it was disinterested, as befits men and women of quality. This attitude to taste was already beyond the moral disapproval of a La Bruyère. By the 1750s it had been recognized for some time that literature, art, and taste had a history, and that taste might be more than merely an aspect of fashion.

Thus by the time the philosophes turned their attention to the arts of their own time and found themselves unable either to approve or to understand them, they had a word at their disposal with which to disown what had become the established artistic norm: *taste*. One could do a great deal by asking: what is good taste? The word might equally well denote a type of judgment or an established convention in the arts; indeed, the word *taste* might be used to question established taste. Obviously, if the philosophes had recourse to taste and the idea of the man of taste, the latter would not be that of baroque society. For among the "men of taste" of that society had been the very amateurs who were now blamed for the decline of the arts, the confusion of taste with luxury, and the false equation of the taste of women with taste tout court. Clearly, if the arts were in decline, and if women dictated taste in the arts, then women could not have real taste; their taste was merely the false taste which ruled society.

The man of taste as represented by Sir Edward Bomston would have a new significance in the world envisaged by the philosophes, Rousseau, and even the economists. Unlike the baroque amateur, *curieux,* or connoisseur, who are tainted by association with passions, the new man of taste seems beyond passion. He asks himself what constitutes good taste, he inquires, like Shaftesbury's virtuoso, as to the true canon of taste, and he will tend to seek that canon in Italy or among the ancients. He may be a man of feelings; but these are dominated by his judgment.

In Diderot's *Rêve de d'Alembert,* Mademoiselle de Lespinasse wonders about the relation of sensibility to taste. She finds herself too sensitive to a play or to music to judge of it, and thinks that reflection upon one's feelings in such a situation may spoil the pleasure taken in a play or an opera. Dr. Bordeu explains that too much sensibility is indeed a hindrance to what we today would call aesthetic pleasure. For to be too moved by a play, or music, or poetry means that the pleasure will pass too quickly for one to be aware of the quality of that pleasure. On the other hand, reflection upon one's pleasure does not, as Mademoiselle de Lespinasse feared, diminish it, but rather augments it. The will must thus intervene to control sensibility, so that one can admire and enjoy without the debilitating effects of pathos. The good critic suspends not so much his disbelief as his sensibility.

Thus the Comte de Saléran became over time a man of taste, in this new philosophical sense. His initial enthusiasm for the arts tore him out of his boredom and the pleasures of dissipation and introduced him to a higher form of pleasure, the refined aesthetic pleasure taken in works of art. Like so much else in the eighteenth century, taste was thus raised up from its former associations and recast as something philosophical. The former pleasures of possession were sublimated into taste. The former accumulators of luxuries were now praised as collectors of taste, whose collections of pictures enriched the national patrimony. And taste not only sublimated the notion of pleasure; it also allowed the separation of the concept of art from luxury.

This philosophizing on the subject of taste is evident not only in the work of the abbé Du Bos and the speculations of Montesquieu, Diderot, Voltaire, Rousseau, and innumerable lesser writers, but also in the thought of Hume, whose discussion of taste is worth closer scrutiny in our attempt to understand the passage from baroque culture to the Enlightenment. Hume clearly presents the man of taste as a philosopher and a type superior to the man of prodigality:

> Philosophers have endeavoured to render happiness entirely independent of everything external. That is

impossible to be *attained:* but every wise man will endeavour to place his happiness on such objects as depend upon himself: and *that* is not to be *attained* so much by any other means as by his delicacy of sentiment. When a man is possessed of that talent, he is more happy by what pleases his taste, than by what gratifies his appetites, and receives more enjoyment from a poem or a piece of reasoning than the most expensive luxury can afford. (*Essays,* 1:4–5)

The need for divertissement and the craving for luxuries are overcome by this delicacy of taste, as taste itself becomes a means to an attainable happiness. At the same time, within the context of eighteenth-century society, the rich man surrounded by his possessions, that hero of luxury associated by Yves Durand with the financier class, is dismissed as a model for emulation. The man of taste belongs to a new elite of the eighteenth century, an elite of culture; for he is "sensible to pains as well as pleasure, which escape the rest of mankind" (1:253). He is beyond ordinary mankind. The effects of delicacy of taste are the same as those of delicacy of passion, that sensibility alluded to by Mademoiselle de Lespinasse, inasmuch as the range of one's feelings is increased in both cases; but the effects of the passions are less harmful. For delicacy of taste is of a higher and more refined nature than mere delicacy of passion; it thus enables man to judge of character, compositions of genius, and works of art. This view of taste and its advantages is a reformulation of the abbé Du Bos's interpretation of the Aristotelian catharsis. But Hume goes beyond Du Bos in his insistence on the *happiness* associated with delicacy of taste. Du Bos wrote in a time still dominated by the taste and values of the age of Louis XIV; Hume is writing for another generation. And happiness, as Saint-Just put it during the Revolution, was a new idea in Europe.

Recalling the metaphor of Pascal's room, one might say that only men and women of taste could remain in that room—which, it must be admitted, had been rendered

more bearable through the interior decoration of the eighteenth century—without a feeling of anxiety or ennui. Taste
thus offered a positive alternative to the Pascalian notion of
divertissement with its negative overtones. And should a
person of taste leave that metaphorical room, it would not
be, as in baroque society, to seek salvation among the Jesuits
or Jansenists, or dissipation at court or town, but for the
pleasures of conversation in some other salon or drawing
room—or, should it be an Englishman taking leave of that
room, it might be for the supposedly higher pleasures of
Italy. "One that has well digested both of books and men,"
writes Hume, "has little enjoyment but in the company of
a few select companions" (1:7). Taste has turned into a form
of wisdom. And as Rousseau perceived, the delicacy of taste
of a Sir Edward Bomston was a sensibility tempered by
stoic wisdom, so that paradoxically the new man of taste
could be defined as a stoic with sensibility.

This delicacy of taste and sensibility tempered by stoicism served not only to distinguish the man of taste from
the majority of mankind, but also from another type rep-
resentative of baroque culture. We have noted that the man
of taste can be distinguished from the amateur and the
curieux; but he can also be distinguished from the man of the
court, the courtier. As Rousseau further describes Sir Edward in *La Nouvelle Héloïse:* "Though he may not possess
that circumspect and reserved politeness based uniquely on
external forms, a politeness which young officers from
France have, he has that of humanity, which prides itself
less on distinguishing rank and status at a glance but generally respects all men" (81). The distinction between a
baroque consideration for form and rank and the supposedly greater and broader conception of humanity in the
Enlightenment could hardly be better put. Sir Edward possesses universal human qualities. The man of taste is defined
as a universal type, a universal ideal, beyond relative, local,
or institutional values. His ancestor in this respect may well
have been the honnête homme of the seventeenth century,

who likewise distinguished himself from the courtier and from other types of the Baroque such as the hero, thus placing himself within the realm of disinterestedness and civility. Yet the greater and finer sensibility of the man of taste of the eighteenth century made for the approval of the philosophes and even Rousseau; whereas the honnête homme had already been exposed by La Bruyère, who discerned in the type more appearance than substance.

·　　·　　·

While the man of taste was defined as a universal type and model for emulation, there remained the question of whether the judgment of taste itself could lay claim to universal validity. To be valid, taste had to be beyond the whims of fashion. If taste was founded on sentiment rather than rules; if, as Hume observed, beauty was not some quality inherent in the object perceived, but lay in the eye of the beholder; if it were truly the case, to quote Shaftesbury, that if "fancy be left judge of anything, she must be judge of all. Every thing is right, if anything be so, because I fancy it" (1:208); then the logical outcome of this subjectivizing of taste (or de-aesthetizing of the concept of taste, as Colin Campbell put it in his brilliant book *The Romantic Ethic and the Spirit of Modern Consumerism*) is philistinism and populism, indeed no standard of taste at all and no man of taste. The eighteenth century solved that dilemma in various ways having nothing to do with logic or history, even before Kant set himself to reconcile subjectivity and universality on the theoretical level. For the question of taste in the eighteenth century could not be and was not separated from questions of culture and class, even if these might go unmentioned.

Thus the late eighteenth century, against all logic and all the evidence of history, assumed the existence of a universal beauty and standard of taste. That it could do this was in part the result of its dismissal of so much of the Baroque as bad taste, mannerism, a departure from the natural, and an effect of the craving for luxuries on the part of the rich and the hated amateurs and the equally disliked role of women in the arts. Taste was not just a subjective preference analogous to the taste of the palate; it was in fact actually good or bad. Nor was it purely a natural trait, a delicate sensibility that an individual might or might not possess; that natural trait could be, indeed had to be, nurtured, trained, and educated. Thus subjective and historical relativism, the latter perceived by Du Bos, Montesquieu, Cartaud de la Vilatte, Voltaire, and others, were bypassed by simply adopting the classical standard of taste and accepting Du Bos's four great ages of taste in history, the Age of Pericles, Augustus, Leo X, and Louis XIV. Horace Walpole might indulge a particular bent for the Middle Ages and still pass as a man of taste, for a man of taste was entitled to amuse himself; but his Gothic castle, Strawberry Hill, was more of a curiosity than a standard of taste for architecture for anyone with true taste. Thus even Hume, who subjectivized taste by displacing beauty from the object to the perceiver, nonetheless appealed to a universal consensus: subjectivity of perception was to be countered by the objectivity of art. "The same Homer, who pleased at Athens and Rome two thousand years ago, is still admired at Paris and London" (1:242). Hume did not say "is still read in Paris and London." Indeed, Pococurante may have been more to the point when he said that the book of Homer dropped from his hands. Nor did Hume bother specifying by whom Homer was admired. For this need not be mentioned; it was assumed that Homer was admired by men of taste, those who had that delicacy of taste to enable them to discern the beauties of Homer even after two thousand years.

The standard of taste in fact rested on certain unstated assumptions. It supposed a class of gentlemen and, within this class, men of taste who were better than ordinary gentlemen precisely because they had taste. The standard of taste also rested on particular works of art, mostly to be found in Italy. In the immortal words of Horace Walpole, "in short, in my opinion, all the qualities of a perfect painter never met but in Raphaël, Guido, and Annibale Carracci" (quoted in Steegman, *The Rule of Taste*, 102). But to know these works also presupposed the grand tour to Italy; furthermore, to these artists (representing the moderns) were to be added the rest of the artistic canon, namely the works of antiquity such as the *Apollo Belvedere*, the *Laocoön*, or the *Discobolus*. Bad taste, judged on this basis, was represented by Bernini and Boucher. Once back from Italy, the English gentleman might want to improve his inherited estate by building a country house in the Palladian manner, which further presupposed a considerable fortune.

Historically considered, this standard of taste leaves out of account the art of the Middle Ages and the very early Renaissance, as well as the Dutch and Flemish school and the French and English schools. This taste was truly *academic*, in the literal sense of the word—the taste of both the French and the English royal academies. But toward this same standard (which is that of a painter like Reynolds) English and French attitudes differed: in France critics attacked it and thereby took aim at the social strata identified with it; but in England it served as a sign of stability, respectability, distinction, and approval. The mob may have its passing fancies, but true men of taste, in the English view, had taste not subject to the vagaries of time and place. "Wherever you can ascertain a delicacy of taste," wrote Hume, "it is sure to meet with approbation; and the best way of ascertaining it is to appeal to those models and principles, which have been established by the uniform consent of nations and ages" (1:242). The Quality (as eighteenth-century England put it in reference to the aristocracy) always recognize quality. The canon of taste was thus also a canon of social merit.

·　　·　　·

Where the Baroque had been inventive in the arts despite the obligation to glorify the powers that be, the new age of sensibility would be conservative and, strictly speaking, even reactionary. For where the baroque artist or poet relied upon imagination to transform models given by the past and thereby create a modern art and poetry and sensibility, and even an entirely new genre such as the opera, the age of taste and sensibility returned to the Greeks and Romans for their supposedly universal models and for the foundations of true taste. Architecture, sculpture, painting, furniture, even dress—all were to be *à l'antique,* which also meant closer to nature. The Baroque had never rejected the Antique in either the arts or literature; but neither Bernini nor Rubens had sacrificed his imagination to a cult of antiquity or an aestheticism such as that formulated by Winckelmann and others. Archaeology had not stifled the imagination.

The Antique played a new role in the age of taste and sensibility of the later eighteenth century. Along with nature, it continued to be the great referent for theory; but it also served as a means of disassociating the Baroque from true taste and thereby distinguishing the concept of art from luxury, and the man of taste from the man of luxury. The amateurs were despised because their departure from the true imitation of the antique forced artists into studio mannerisms and deviation from true taste in order to please the amateurs. True taste and true art were not to be found in the exhibitions of the salon, the hôtels of the opulent, the churches of the Jesuits, or even the palaces of kings. True art and true taste lay elsewhere: in Italy, in Sicily, in ancient Rome, in ancient Greece, and even further east in Syria and Egypt. The true taste of Italy, however, was not that of modern Italy or Sicily, but only that taste discernible in the ruins of ancient Rome and those works assembled in the collections of antiquarians. Whereas the Baroque had produced an art inseparable from life, the inspiration for true taste already came from the museum. The museum age had yet to be born, but it was only a few years off.

Taste thus acquired a meaning it had not had at the time of the abbé Du Bos or Hume. For Du Bos, taste meant the taste of the *gens du monde,* the men and women of society, who judged on the basis of an informed pleasure and sentiment, rather than by rules as had the pedants of the seventeenth century. These men and women might even include amateurs and women of luxury. But between Du Bos and Hume, and even between Hume and Winckelmann and Diderot as the rich became more and more visible and their influence on the arts more pronounced and their luxury more striking, the notion of taste, seen now as something associated with the antique and a certain stoic wisdom, took on a significance beyond the purely aesthetic. For one thing, delicacy of taste offered greater pleasure than luxury and for that reason alone was something superior to wealth, luxury, and "consumption" as this last functioned in the Paris and London of the eighteenth century. At the same time, taste could bring discipline to luxury. The rich who would be seen and gaped at by the mob, the rich who would show off their wealth through profligacy and confuse appearance with substance, no longer awed the elite. Society now required more than mere wealth for a man to be considered a person of quality: culture and taste had become prerequisites. The man of taste had thus risen beyond a dependence on externals. He was a philosophe and, to use Veblen's later term, beyond invidious comparisons.

Of course, the man of taste could not be a poor man. What is left unsaid by Hume and all other writers on taste and the arts, with the possible exception of the far less diplomatic Monsieur Necker, is that, as we noted with Hume, delicacy of taste presupposes wealth, leisure, and ease. But wealth in itself did not make the man of taste; nor could it be bought.

As a concept, taste was based on considerations which presumably stood apart from economics, power, or even social preeminence. The concept rested instead on that newly discovered realm of the period, the aesthetic. This was a new word, but the phenomenon it alluded to had existed before, as a *certo non so che* or *je ne sais quoi*—terms frequently used in the seventeenth century when rational explanation failed to account for some pleasure taken in a work of art or some charm of manner or wit, or perhaps the charm of a woman at court or in town who, though not considered a beauty, had a certain something which pleased, one knew not why.

In this continuity from the *je ne sais quoi* to the aesthetic and taste it becomes possible to see that what is considered aesthetic—that which escapes precise definition by reason, common sense, nature or necessity, in short that which seems gratuitous—may well be a constant in society. Thus in the Enlightenment, considered as the century of philosophy or the age of reason, the aesthetic represents a survival of the baroque. The mentality of the elite may no longer have been baroque, to be sure, what with the emphasis on utilitarianism and economics and the reform of the state; but this does not preclude the survival of baroque traits, as is the case even with our society. The man of taste, in this changing eighteenth century, represented a new elite of the refined within a world of other elites: the court, the rich, the old country nobility, the members of prestigious academies, the professionals of law and medicine. Taste created the cultural elite of the Enlightenment. And since the standard of taste, like human nature itself, was decreed to be universal and was discussed in universal terms, the elite which taste represented was thought to be beyond rank, estate, and class. The man of taste was the counterpole to that other new man of the eighteenth century, the economic man. The man of taste rose beyond luxury and mere wealth to a new and higher principle of existence; from this new height he might pass judgment on all previous tastes, as well as on amateurs, connoisseurs, *curieux,* dilettantes, and the ostentatious and prodigal rich. His luxury was not that of ostentation, either of objects or of knowledge, but that *luxe de mollesse* which partook of the pleasures of nature and simplicity and humanity. *Nil admirari,* the man of taste judged dispassionately of what we call the Baroque and the Rococo, and ultimately of his own taste too, thereby rising in a sense even beyond taste to philosophy.

Rousseau's Emile is precisely such a man. Rousseau did not fail to cultivate Emile's taste, that is, his innate faculty for judging of that which pleases and displeases not only the greatest number of men, but also that much smaller number who comprise the elite of taste. Rousseau was, to judge from book 4 of *Emile,* very well read in the matter of taste. He was aware of the difficulty of defining it, of explaining the reasons for a judgment of taste in the arts, as he was aware that it was relative to mores, history, geography, character, sex, and institutions. Taste depended on one's sensibility and on the cultivation of that sensibility. Now in order to cultivate one's natural given taste, one's faculty of judgment, it was best to live in a populous society, for the acquisition of taste depended on the range of comparisons one could make. It was also best to live in a society devoted to leisure and amusement, because a society devoted to business was motivated by the search for profit rather than the search for pleasure. And it was best to live in a society where inequality was not too pronounced, where the tyranny of opinion was moderate, and where sensuality reigned rather than vanity—where, in other words, one sought pleasure rather than distinction. In fact, Rousseau was describing Paris as it was in his day for a certain elite.

Of course, this did not mean that Paris was a model of good taste. Far from it. Yet Rousseau would educate Emile precisely in Paris, even though there was probably no city in which the general taste was worse. But the place was bursting with thought, wit, and stimulation of every description; there one might learn to think and to compare, and one might survive the bad taste by invoking contrasting examples. Emile would be set to read the ancients and would soon learn to appreciate their simplicity, manliness, and natural qualities over against the products of modern

taste. He would thus have surmounted the bad taste of the
present to attain to the good taste already shown by the
ancients. But good taste was more than just something
associated with the arts or letters; it was beyond riches.
"The man of taste and true pleasure," writes Rousseau,
"does not need riches; it is enough for him to be free and
the master of himself" (*Emile,* end of bk. 4). And it is not
the least of the paradoxes of that revolutionary writer that,
in his speculations on what he would do were he rich, he
should have posited the life and home of the country gentleman as an aesthetic ideal. The man of taste turns into a
philosophe who ends up looking remarkably like landed
gentry. One thinks of Voltaire at Ferney as much as of
Rousseau's Monsieur de Wolmar at Clarens.

Changing Appearances:
From Court to Beau Monde

The redefinition of taste was not only the philosophical
result of a will to distinguish art from luxury. It may well
have also been prompted by the rise of another phenomenon inseparable from luxury, indeed made possible by
increased wealth and luxury, namely *fashion,* which, like
economics and aesthetics, also achieved its autonomy with
the decline of baroque society. The significance of fashion
in the course of the eighteenth century thus merits a digression that may help to answer the questions raised above
when we wondered whether eighteenth-century Parisian
society was or was not a proto–consumer society.

Around 1755, Rousseau, prompted in part by his very
real sickness but also by moral considerations inseparable
from appearances, decided to reform his life. He began with
a reform of his appearance, to bring it into correspondence
with his self, his true being: "I began my reform with my
dress; I quit gold gilding and white stockings, took on a
round wig, gave up my sword, sold my watch, telling

myself with incredible joy: Thank Heaven I shall no longer need to know what time it is" (*Confessions,* bk. 8, 363). Rousseau's change of appearance signaled his resolution to break the fetters of opinion and fashion and to live in independence and poverty rather than continue wearing a mask, the mask required by polite society and one which the philosophes were willing to assume even while condemning the baroque society epitomized by that mask. Diderot, as Rousseau later realized, after they had gone their separate ways, had become a *monsieur.* Rousseau, whatever his success, still felt himself of the people, certainly not at ease in Parisian society, and he would dress accordingly, as dictated by his health and sentiments rather than by fashion. As for the watch he gave up, it was a gesture pointing to another aspect of fashion: the regulation of social appearances, calls to be made, obligations to be seen at certain places and at certain times. Time, one might say, regulated entrances and exits in the world just as it did changes of scene on stage.

Rousseau's gesture may seem revolutionary from our present-day perspective; to his philosophical acquaintances it was simply madness. One may, however, also argue that is was a profoundly conservative, even reactionary, gesture, for it implicitly accepted the traditional requirement that appearances correspond to being. Rousseau thus pointed to a baroque society gone wrong because appearances no longer corresponded to reality. Dress in baroque society, ever since the early seventeenth century and the first appearance of satires on fashion, had oscillated between two poles, stability and fashion, with fashion invariably associated with change. Both luxury and fashion thus constituted threats to the assumed correspondence between appearance and being, and therefore to the stability of society. The comic element in Molière's *Bourgeois gentilhomme* derives from the gap between Monsieur Jourdain's pretensions and his being—between what he would appear to be with the help of his tailor, his master of arms, his philosophy tutor, and his dancing master, and what in reality he was born to be, a well-off commoner in trade. From the point of view of baroque society, pretensions to quality threatened the correspondence between appearance and reality on which the social world was founded. Political, social, religious, and artistic considerations required that in baroque society everyone remain in his or her God-given station and look as if he or she did indeed belong there.

This relation of appearance to being was nothing if not the general aesthetic principle of *convenance,* linked to *bienséance,* or decorum, and even to verisimilitude. It is obvious that while baroque society may have taken its justification from religion, it ultimately rested on merely aesthetic principles. It is the aesthetic and social discrepancy between appearance and being which made for the innumerable comic and ambiguous moral situations of the novels and plays of the period, and of course in real life as well. What made Casanova, a commoner of dubious extraction, possible was precisely the power which imagination as fashion exercised in the face of evidence to the contrary. He was fashionable, and he appeared and played his role in fashionable society, a new scene which appeared in the course of the eighteenth century, a scene different from that of the court yet an offshoot of it, and by the end of the century unmistakably cosmopolitan. Curiously enough, even Rousseau, for all his antisocial gestures, would also become fashionable, too much so for his peace of mind and the repose of his body. In the eighteenth century as in our own time, "the system," here fashion, had a way of absorbing even its opponents. The power of fashion was such that it transformed the old baroque court society into what we may call the *beau monde.* The change becomes evident in the art of portraiture.

·   ·   ·

The grand flowering of the portrait in the baroque testifies to the age's belief in the importance of appearances even when it was suspicious of appearances. For the age believed that appearances ought to be in harmony with being, with reality; it distrusted appearances only because it knew that this was not always the case. Thus kings ought to look like kings, princes ought to look princely, the great of this world ought to look their part, and so on down the social scale. Where there was no or little correspondence between appearance and reality, between nature and the ideal, then art might correct and improve on nature. Thus if a king did not look very kingly, as with Charles I of England, then a Van Dyck might very well improve upon the king and produce a representation which made him truly look the part of the realm's First Gentleman. Louis XIV was lucky enough to be a handsome youth and to look the part he was born to; similarly Louis XV, though not Louis XVI. As for the Hapsburgs of both Austria and Spain, despite their chins and lips, a Titian or a Velázquez left no one in doubt as to what they were: the emperor looked like an emperor and the king like a king. Even ministers like the Count-Duke of Olivares and Cardinal Richelieu were represented with the grandeur, dignity, and gravity befitting their high office. The very idea of monarchy thus found its emblematic representation in the official standing portrait with its by-now-familiar attributes—the crown, the scepter, the grand column, the billowing curtains, the sword of Charlemagne for Louis XIV—while the equestrian portrait made of the king a leader of armies, a conqueror, a hero.

Attributes as signs of rank might extend from the highest echelons of society down to the lowest rank still worthy of being represented for the public gaze. And as Diderot, following Montesquieu, perceived, each rank had its own air, its own attitudes, its own expression, determined not only by the conventions of art but also by its position in society and the form of that society—monarchy, republic, despotism. Princes, bishops, dukes, and lesser ranks all had to look their part. But it was apparent, too, that the merely

rich might also, by art, be made to look grand and princely.
Thus the wealthy Samuel Bernard, who was privileged to
lend money to Louis XIV, had himself portrayed with the
same grand column and billowing curtains as a prince
would, though to signify his earthly role the painter did not
neglect to include a globe and a fleet of ships to point out
Bernard's grand commercial interests. Monarchs, like
popes and saints, might also be portrayed in their moment
of apotheosis, rising to the heavens where angels awaited
their coming; or monarchs might be portrayed accompanied by the allegorical figures of certain virtues which, as
some contemporary observers did not fail to note, they did
not personally possess. Then there were the beauties of the
court, who might also be portrayed, and beautified, as
muses or pagan deities that no one believed in.

By the mid–eighteenth century these conventional portraits had been reduced to just that, a convention of limited
appeal and interest. The art of portraiture in this manner had
reached a certain limit. For the true type of Enlightenment
portraiture one must look elsewhere.

The allegorical portrait was of course already a departure
from the baroque-Christian moral requirement of the conformity of appearance to being. But this was a mere game,
a play of the fancy, somewhat as the opera was a free play
of the fancy. Verisimilitude was kept to a minimum. But
together with the critique of opera, of poetic imagination,
and of luxury, there also came an associated critique of
baroque dress, in the name of both nature and health—and
this was bound to affect the art of portraiture. Increasingly
over the course of the eighteenth century it was no longer
the court alone which set the tone and presumably determined those appearances which were supposed to correspond to being. The call for a more natural model, and the
influence of the town, both began to play a role in the
creation of appearances. Fashion, in short, began to deter-
mine the representation of men, women, and children, thus
in effect altering the relation of appearance to being. Where

Van Dyck had improved upon nature to make Charles look like a king, the portraitists of the eighteenth century were called upon not so much to make sitters look their rank as to make them appear in harmony with something far more fluid and undefinable: the need to look fashionable. One might say that in the course of the century the town rivaled and eventually triumphed over the court by creating "society," even when "society" left town for its summer houses and châteaux in the country. By the end of the eighteenth century, court and town were united as participants in a new spectacle: society and its ever-varying fashions. And not only did fashion create fashionable portraitists, but the portraitists in turn created a fashion and made it known abroad—for fashion required a whole host of portraitists and draftsmen and engravers to spread its own creations.

In this long and by no means uniform transformation of portraiture, the roles of Reynolds and Gainsborough are of particular importance. It may well be that in England the influence of the court was weaker in matters of taste and fashion than in France, so that English society was less obliged to follow the court. Gainsborough and Reynolds would find their French equivalent later in the work of Madame Vigée-Lebrun, but for the moment they were innovators of appearance: they invented appearances as fashion rather than as representations of rank. Fashion might be described as the result of life dominated by the imagination and imitating art—which is not the same thing as rank submitting to artistic conventions of representation in order to embody the idea of what a king, a duke, a count, a great magistrate, or a hero ought to look like, so that appearance is made to correspond to being, to substance.

Thus when Reynolds adapts certain poses gleaned from antique statuary to the modern Englishman or when Gainsborough adapts Van Dyck dress and style to modern men and women, they are creating not a representation of rank in the baroque manner, as Rigaud or Rubens or Velázquez did, but a new appearance not necessarily corresponding to any supposed substance or being or rank. They are creating pure appearance, what we call an *image*. What critics of baroque portraiture had seen as mere convention and illusion, discord between appearance and being, was here replaced by illusion of a new sort, one which conveyed the appearance of naturalness rather than observing the obligations and rules of representation imposed by rank. A lord need not appear as a lord, but as a man of fashion; a duchess need not appear as the Duchess of Devonshire, but as a lady of fashion. This shift was not gratuitous, for fashion dictated naturalness—a naturalness which was enhanced by the park backgrounds, the children, sometimes the melancholy of certain feminine portraits, as well as color, pose, and costume. Fashion replaced the representation of rank, which presupposed a social hierarchy, with a new creation, one which lifted those represented out of the social to a new realm of existence: distinction. These new portraits made visible the aesthetic elite.

In his 1925 work, *La Barrière et le niveau,* the French philosopher Goblot perceived distinction to be that which characterized the nineteenth-century French bourgeoisie. For him, distinction was a separate category, a separate trait, from the aesthetic. The aesthetic, in his view, remained linked to the beautiful; thus he associated the old nobility with the aesthetic and the bourgeoisie with distinction. In truth, if he had considered portraiture from the Baroque through the end of the eighteenth century, he might have discerned his category of distinction in the making and come to see that here, as in so many other matters of social usage, the bourgeoisie was merely imitating the old nobility.

With Reynolds, Gainsborough, Vigée-Lebrun, Lawrence, and Gilbert Stuart, portraiture enters into the system of fashion, which gains its autonomy over the course of the eighteenth century. Montesquieu, as early as his *Lettres persanes* of 1721, had perceived that luxury begets fashion, which begets distinction, which saps the stability of the social hierarchy. When a chambermaid can look like a duchess, social stability is threatened; but comedy is possible. It is precisely this drive for distinction that in portraiture means individuation and makes of the eighteenth century portrait such a rich source of interest and enjoyment. This adaptation of art to the creation of the new appearance makes for an element of aestheticism which is inseparable from the work of certain British portraitists who depicted high society. Reynolds in the Academy and in his *Discourses* may have sought to maintain the true taste of the grand manner, but in fact he lived off fashion. Dandyism was not far off.

As a result of the power of fashion, court society in the eighteenth century was gradually displaced by a new creation: the beau monde. If the courtier, the honnête homme, the English gentleman, the hero, and perhaps even the newly arrived philosophe might all represent baroque types, what, given the critique of appearances, would be the new man and woman represented in the new portraiture? We have said they would be given more individuality than their forebears; but one can nevertheless also see them as representing a new type. Historically speaking, there is no doubt that they do in fact represent the new elite of the eighteenth century, as distinct from the old nobility. What then do they have in common?

One is tempted to say, borrowing from the Physiocrats but giving the word a different meaning, "class"—class, in other words, as we still use the term today, as something standing apart from economic considerations. The new elite was no longer founded on inherited rank or mere title but on wealth and accomplishment, and what the portraits of this new elite do, in effect, is to give wealth and accomplishment "class." It is one thing to be rich, quite another to have class. The instrument used to confer this "class" was fashion, as the beau monde supplanted the court as general model for society. The painters of this new beau monde were Madame Vigée-Lebrun, Sir Thomas Lawrence, Gilbert Stuart, and others. They managed to give this new elite an air of naturalness, affability, civility, and ease, so that one quite naturally and without question accepted their ruling position in society and their distinction from the generality of mankind recently declared to be born equal and endowed with natural rights. Appearances had, despite philosophical criticism, once again triumphed over reality. Daniel Roche in his book on dress in the seventeenth and eighteenth centuries, *La Culture des apparences,* sums up the trend as follows:

> During the seventeenth and eighteenth centuries, among the higher classes, ornament and finery dictate masculine and feminine habits and a maximum of artificiality and decorative increase. A quarter of a century before the Revolution, philosophical criticism denounces the generalized excesses of fashion and aristocratic consumption in the name of Nature, which results in imposing the artificiality of the natural which is anything but economical. (51)

For Roche, the old baroque problem of the correspondence between appearance and being is resolved through the rise of fashion and its eventual autonomy in the triumph of appearances. Might this then imply that by 1789 society was more baroque than ever—that the Baroque had in fact triumphed over the Enlightenment?

•   •   •

If, as historians would have it, baroque society was the solution to the general crisis of the seventeenth century, then fashion was the fatal flaw within the structure of the Baroque. As Maravall has pointed out, innovation was blocked in religion, in politics, in law, even in science and technology in some countries, and consequently could thrive only in artistic and poetic caprice. Novelty in the arts hid the lack of it in the social structure and the power structure: "Passion for the outlandish, where it was permitted, developed monstrously among peoples who found their ways blocked to a rational criticism of social life" (*Culture of the Baroque,* 229). The Enlightenment critique of modern life, of society, of established customs and tastes, hardly eradicated the outlandish: the freedom of imagination inherited from baroque fantasy was now perceived in negative terms, in both art and fashion—in the arts as decadence, in fashion as something unnatural and unhealthy. Fashion thus continued to be seen by Christian moralists, now seconded by philosophes and economists, as opposed to reason and nature, and as frivolity, caprice, and excess. The author of the article "Mode" in the *Encyclopédie* could thus write that "fashions destroy and succeed each other sometimes without the least appearance of reason, the bizarre often being preferred to the beautiful simply because it is novel" (quoted by Roche, 435). Thus, the *Encyclopédie* author continues, when a rhinoceros turned up in Europe, probably the one painted by Pietro Longhi in Venice, there was not a woman without three or four such creatures upon her as ornamentation; later these same women would be rushing about town to get a bonnet *au lapin, au zéphir, au cupidon, à la comète,* or what have you.

Had the article "Mode" been written in the 1780s, its author might also have mentioned the *coiffure à la Junon,* to wit, a coiffure decorated with a model of the frigate *Juno,* which had participated in the American War of Independence. For hairdressing was one art which triumphed over nature even after Rousseau. Marie Antoinette paid her fashionable hairdresser Leonard 1,574 livres for his work in 1784 and allowed him to dress the hair of other ladies, so that he was soon the favorite choice to dress one's hair for court receptions. Here the Baroque survived with all its fantastic freedom of expression intact. Some elaborate constructions had to be prepared the day before the reception, thus forcing the ladies to sleep sitting up or standing the night before the event so as not to disturb these magnificent artefacts. Some coiffures were decorated with real flowers, which drew water from glass vials hidden within their complicated structures. Others sported mechanical birds which might be set to trill. And there was one type of coiffure, called *à la grand-mère,* which might be raised or lowered at will by a mechanical device in case an overly lofty headdress alarmed some elderly lady. One might thus say that just as the last fireworks at court were the manifestations of a surviving baroque art form—a typically ephemeral art form—so these fantastic coiffures were likewise a surviving manifestation of baroque play, caprice, fantasy, and imagination.

Despite its excesses, to follow fashion had become an obligation for higher society and for those who wished, on a more modest level of expense, to follow in its wake. The life of society came to be regulated by the vicissitudes of fashion, affecting not only dress and coiffure but also pleasures and amusements, places to be, things or persons to see, events to be attended. Parisian and London society became a spectacle which already had its taste setters. In the Paris of Louis XVI those who set the tone were the queen herself, her friend the Duchesse de Polignac, the Comte de Vaudreuil, the king's brother the Comte d'Artois, and Duc d'Orleans, and generally the fashionable beauties portrayed by Madame Vigée-Lebrun, herself a fashionable artist. But then even Benjamin Franklin was fashionable; after all, he was so very different.

What under Louis XIII, Charles I, Louis XIV, and Charles II had still served to represent the grandeur of monarchy had thus, by the end of the eighteenth century, turned into pure appearance with no corresponding being. As Roche points out, fashion had become an autonomous phenomenon. It was considered frivolous by critics of luxury and by moralists, but it was in fact far from frivolous, since it allowed the individual to free him- or herself from the constraints of rank and hierarchy. It was also, if we follow Roche, the manifestation of a new type of culture which was largely invented for and by women.

The second half of the eighteenth century saw in France the flowering of a new type of literature, the fashion magazine. There had been satirical accounts of fashion since its beginnings in court society, but with the eighteenth century fashion prompted a far more serious type of literature. The fashion press was created by men for women, though it was sometimes also written by women. The most successful of these magazines was the *Cabinet des modes,* which was first published by the Parisian bookseller François Buisson in 1785. The following year it was renamed, significantly, the *Magasin des modes nouvelles françaises et anglaises,* signaling in effect the arrival of English fashion in France. From 1790 to 1793 this same magazine appeared as the *Journal de la mode et du goût.* This was the longest-lived of such journals, which appeared prolifically for greater or lesser spans of time after the 1750s and which in essence constituted a feminine press. The *Journal des dames,* for example, found readers from Cadiz to St. Petersburg, from Stockholm to Naples. It was a literature differing from both the literature of the Enlightenment and the low-life literature discerned by Robert Darnton. The literature of the Enlightenment, as Roche points out, produced books and writings on the sciences, arts, and philosophy; the provincial press continued to produce a good number of religious titles. What the feminine press produced showed a greater interest in belles lettres, theater, poetry, and novels—in short, a leisure culture that was also entirely lay.

This feminine culture of leisure, fashion, and taste in effect contributed, as did the Enlightenment in its own way, to undermining the foundations of the traditional hierarchies of society. For this was a culture which stressed an ethic of pleasure and a life given over to the cultivation of the agreeable arts. In this regard the new feminine culture was squarely at odds with the ethic of the economists. Indeed the economists had indirectly criticized this culture as part of their general critique of luxury even before it was singled out as specifically feminine. This new feminine culture was inseparable from the publicity given to objects of consumption, even if such publicity was still restricted to the higher levels of society. In short, from the point of view of the critics of luxury, fashion was merely one special aspect of it, one which implied yet another form of deficit spending.

Traditional baroque society, we may suggest, is one in which appearances must correspond to being; a consumer society is one in which there are only appearances; and a bourgeois society is one in which appearance is dictated by one's budget, which the bourgeois likes to see balanced. If we follow Roche's examination of dress in the seventeenth and eighteenth centuries, it becomes evident that by the 1780s the upper layers of the social pyramid had all the earmarks of a consumer society, with consumption evident above all in fashion—whence the significance of his title, *The Culture of Appearances.* From an economist's point of view this culture was the result of baroque spending, and over the course of the century the requirements of fashion drove a good part of the nobility of court and town, that is, of Paris, to overspend on appearance. The obligation to spend, once restricted to the nobility, had by now spread downward to the lesser levels of society. Deficit spending on dress was thus no longer dictated by rank alone, but by the far more capricious requirements of fashion. Dress was the most expensive item among consumer goods, not only because it had to be replaced due to wear, but also because it was subject to the variations of fashion, the tug-of-war between stability and current fashionability. Some favored stability and opted for modesty, though of course within the bounds of acceptable appearance; others opted to follow the fashion no matter what the cost or their budget. Thus the Montesquiou family, singled out as one example by Roche, was from 1780 to 1793 almost constantly running a deficit. Not all nobles spent in this manner, to be sure— witness the Schombergs, who maintained an equilibrium between their budget and the requirements of appearance— and in the provinces the requirements of fashion were far less expensive than in Paris. What is of interest in the case of the Montesquious, the Polignacs, and others close to Marie-Antoinette is that precisely here baroque spending met its splendid apotheosis . . . in the red. In Roche's words: "Fashion thus appears under its multiple faces, animator of change, magician of distinction, creator of social equality, stage manager of inequalities of appearance" (476).

During the Revolution there were a few attempts to create a national costume which would restore the old relation of appearance and being, but this attempt had no chance of success. With the Directoire, fashion regained its old dominance over a renewed society; appearance would henceforth be determined by autonomous fashion and the requirements, not of rank, but of distinction. Looking back then upon the tensions between the Enlightenment and the Baroque, between art and luxury, luxury and taste, frugality and baroque spending, we can see that the end of baroque society, taken as an aesthetically unified society in which appearance must correspond to being, implied the rise of three different autonomies: economics, aesthetics, and, last but by no means least, fashion. Kant's careful distinction between aesthetic art and the merely pleasurable arts may be more readily understood within the context of a time in which fashion was at odds with art, reason, and true taste, and still perceived by moralists, economists, and philosophers as frivolity.

Conclusion:
The End of the Baroque
and the Invention of Aesthetic Art

In the baroque imagination as projected onto the vaults and ceilings of churches, saints and martyrs were seen to rise amidst clouds and angels to the heavens, where they might contemplate the Father, the Son, and the Holy Ghost in bliss eternal. And in the secular realm, the ceilings of palaces and town houses or hôtels also proclaimed the glory and triumph of the great of this world. In the social order imagined by the philosophes and the economists, one might still hope for a statue to some great benefactor of mankind adorning a public square; but ceilings could no longer be decorated by fictions. For the whole of the Baroque, after an initial denial, would be transfigured and allowed to rise to a new empyrean, whose gods would be represented in temples called museums. The new secular empyrean was the realm of aesthetic art, and what had once been decried as luxury was therein transfigured into the icons of a secular transcendence, as the signs of human destiny.

•   •   •

By 1789 the imagination of the ruling elite of court and town had been so thoroughly secularized that any new signs of its beliefs could only be secular. The early eighteenth-century standard of taste, which might still ascribe canonical status to the Bolognese masters, had come by the end of the century to be dismissed by the enthusiasts of the Antique as an aberration. True taste was *à l'antique* all over Europe; the words *baroque* and *rococo,* when used, were used as terms of disdain, and the style of Louis XV and Madame de Pompadour dismissed as *chicorée.* Madame du Barry, who was not Madame de Pompadour, preferred the rather insipid but fashionable "Greek" style of Vien to the *fêtes galantes* of Fragonard. To be sure, the Antique was still only one of various possible manners, though critics and some artists were persuaded it was the true manner. But the Revolution would make of it the style par excellence of the Republic and of true art.

At the same time, the Revolution also posed the question of what to do with all the accumulated luxury of the ancien régime, a luxury decried for a whole century by philosophes, moralists, and economists. The discourse against luxury and for art had been couched in universals: one wrote on beauty, the sublime, imitation, taste, and genius as if works of art were separate from luxury and the signs of wealth and power. But in the course of the Revolution there were those among the people who read works of art and luxury precisely as being the signs of tyranny and oppression, and as such many were defaced and destroyed. The notion that works of art and monuments were signs had by 1789 entered into ordinary discourse, to play an important role in the course of the Revolution.

As for the signs of ostentatious luxury, these were put on the market. On 25 August 1793, there began a sale of over 17,000 items from the Château de Versailles, a sale that lasted for an entire year. A part of the Baroque was be'.g liquidated. Some precious furniture was saved wh~.i the king was transferred to Paris; more was saved by the government of the Directory; the rest has been scattered to the four corners of the earth. But before it was sold, something

else of significance happened to this furniture that had been
such an integral part of baroque splendor and luxury. It was
classified. Those left in charge of the château when the king
left for Paris in October 1789 drew up an inventory. The
objects of ostentatious luxury thus were reduced to items in
a list of holdings, items of property; those who were in
charge of the château became, in a sense, curators and
registrars. The age of liberty came into existence hand in
hand with that of property and administration.

But not everyone wanted to destroy the signs of tyranny.
Even if the arts were the signs of tyranny, they were also
something more: they were now a national patrimony and
the product of the national genius, the heritage of the people
and nation. Hence the importance of the museum. The
Muséum du Louvre was born of a decree of 19 September
1792.

The idea of creating a museum in the Louvre was an old
one. But there is a clear discontinuity of intention between
the plans for such a museum as conceived in the administration of the Comte d'Angiviller, Director of the King's
Buildings, and what was instituted after the fall of the
monarchy. As Jean-Rémy Mantion has shown in his contribution to *La Carmagnole des Muses,* the museum of the
monarchy was very different from that of the Republic. The
museum envisaged during the reign of Louis XVI by d'Angiviller, Pierre, Hubert Robert, and others was to be a
temple to the muses and the arts, but it was not conceived
as a space for public exhibitions. It was to be for the royal
collections, and as such was also a monument to the glory
and patronage of Louis XVI. Such a museum would be
completely in line with the development of aesthetic thinking over the course of the eighteenth century, the recog-
nition of genius, talent, and art as the signs of national
history. It would have signaled at last a separation of art
from luxury, and might have answered to the requirement
of philosophes and critics and even amateurs to render
proper homage to the arts.

There are few indications, according to Mantion, as to what this museum might have looked like had it been built. Jean-Jacques La Grenée painted an allegorical picture of the museum and presented it at the Salon of 1783, but the painting itself has not survived. All that is left is a prose description of it from the exhibition catalogue:

> Near the pedestal on which may be seen the bust of the king, Immortality receives from the hands of Painting, Justice, and Benevolence the portrait of the Count d'Angiviller, to be placed in his Temple. Behind the figure of Immortality, the Genius of the Arts lifts a curtain, and one may see the Grande Galerie where several little genii transport and place the king's pictures. (Quoted in Mantion, 100)

There is, however, one visual item which conveys an intimation of the proposed museum, namely a drawing attributed to Boullée. It shows a rotunda, with the king's statue in the center, two guards at the entrance, statues in front of columns supporting the rotunda's dome, and on the wall behind the columns oval-framed paintings which are probably portraits. The museum portrayed here is indeed dedicated to French art. But neither the prose description nor the drawing depicts the museum as it was later to be built. Indeed, they suggest a national monument—something which would have been approved not only by d'Angiviller and the king but by Mercier and the other philosophes as well. Mercier would have preferred history pictures to portraits; still, if the portraits were of great men it would not have displeased the philosophic party.

The new museum was to be erected in the Louvre, and thus the arrival of Louis XVI in the Louvre in 1789 takes on particular significance. For when the king was assigned the Louvre as residence, it was as if he and the monarchy were in effect already in a museum: the king was part of the collection. This was not lost on some of his contemporaries.

For the deputy Barrère, Versailles had been the palace of despotism, where the king had gone to hide from the gaze of the people and to surround himself with luxury. In returning to the Louvre, according to Barrère, the king was not thinking of the Louvre merely as a place of residence, but as palace of the arts and home of the sciences, which would honor his sojourn there in its capacity as the visible sign of the majesty of the nation. Remove the king from the Louvre entirely, as after August 1792, and it could become a new type of museum altogether.

Through the creation of the Muséum du Louvre, the work of art became part of the heritage of the nation. The task of the museum was to acquire and preserve the works of the ancien régime scattered across the land in palaces, hôtels, and châteaux. But it was soon realized that the creation of the museum implied more than the gathering and preserving of works of art, and that an ongoing discussion had also been initiated. The museum was now also conceived as an educational institution, and an inspiration for the new art which would be worthy of the Republic. The eighteenth-century obsession with luxury was a thing of the past, but the question of the definition of art and of what should be put into the museum and displayed therein had only begun. As David put it, "Do not be mistaken. Citizens, the museum is not a vain accumulation of objects of luxury and frivolity, serving to satisfy curiosity" (quoted in Mantion, 108). Rather, the museum must become a school of the arts, nurture genius, inspire new masterpieces.

But could one avoid the museum's turning into an accumulation of objects of luxury and frivolity to satisfy the merely curious? Was it so certain that the problem of luxury had been effectively and finally solved? Or was it merely that a new type of art had been created, adhering to a new type of luxury?

What in the late baroque culture had been intimately and institutionally linked to power, glory, and wealth and criticized as prodigality and luxury was now, as we have seen, sold on the auction block, collected, and put in museums. But once in museums these objects, once dismissed as baubles or images of superstition, underwent a strange transformation. They were transfigured. If the transfer of the Sistine Madonna from its original convent to the collection of Augustus the Strong had transformed that painting from an object of religion into an object of art for the enjoyment of the king and others who saw it, then the transfer of such an object to a museum meant a further transformation. The transfer from the monastery to the king had meant a transit through the art market: the picture that had served religion had become an object of beauty but also an object of luxury. The transfer of such an object to the museum stripped it of its quality of luxury. Thus was born that new category, as yet unnamed: museum art. The works of the past acquired an aura, that of the aesthetic, of high art, of the never-to-be-again. And as signs of the past, they took on not only a historical significance but also, thanks to the aesthetic aura, a kind of transcendent meaning: they were the works of human destiny.

The end of the Baroque thus implied the etherealization of the concept of art, its purification and dissociation from mere luxury, mere entertainment, and mere desire, the distancing of art from the hated amateurs, the frivolous *curieux,* the pretentious connoisseurs, the fashionable women, and the idle rich. Art was preserved—but at what price? Was this aesthetic art still alive? Or was it a dead art? David's friend Quatremère de Quincy, one-time sculptor turned antiquarian, was in no doubt as to the answer. For him the art of museums, the transfer of works of art from their original intended site to some museum, implied breaking the link that had always existed between creations of genius and society, between art and mores, art and religion, art and life. Art in museums might well be beyond the art market, but objects in museums were still regarded as precious, as objects of speculation, of finicky research and finicky taste, as material rather than spiritual objects. Their function was gone. Their meaning was lost. They were objects behind glass, unconnected with the life of society about them—art split off from life, or as John Dewey would later put it, in a society whose arts began with the museum age, art split off from experience.

Given this split, the new judgment of taste could well be characterized as disinterested.

.   .   .

When the abbé Du Bos published his *Réflexions critiques sur la poésie et la peinture* in 1719, he wrote as an inheritor of baroque culture. His context, his experience of the arts and society, was thus rather different from that of Immanuel Kant, who published his *Critique of Judgment* at the end of the Enlightenment. When the abbé Du Bos wrote that the public judged of a work of art *disinterestedly,* he meant that the vanity, jealousy, prejudices, or rivalries of the artists were not involved in that judgment, nor for that matter any pedantic regard for the supposed rules of art on the part of scholarly critics. Professionals involved in the arts tended to judge in terms of rival claims and various prejudices; their judgment was thus apt to be "interested" in that they were, so to speak, caught up in the arena of judgment, in the play, poem, or picture being judged. They had a vested interest in the outcome of the game. The public, on the other hand, judged on the basis of its pleasure or displeasure with the work; this judgment was disinterested in the sense that the public was not involved personally in the work's success or failure. An aristocratic or noble public of the arts was above the disputes of pedants or the quarrels of poets or musicians. Du Bos wrote still within the sphere of the aesthetics of pleasure. And when Du Bos discusses this disinterested judgment of taste, the reader is left in no doubt as to who exercises such judgment. The public are the *gens du monde;* the context may be the opera, the theater, a gallery, a salon, even a reader and his book.

With Kant, at the end of the century, it is not really clear who exercises a disinterested aesthetic judgment, nor when, nor within what context. But the definition of that judgment has been refined. Not only is the judgment of taste disinterested, it is "aesthetic," that is, free of desire—just as the beautiful, object of that judgment, is also defined as the result of a purpose without purposefulness, as its own end and finality. The judgment of taste as conceived and formulated by Kant comes to be something otherworldly, the taste, so to speak, of angels, angels without desires, angels with an objective subjectivity, making subjective judgments which nevertheless can lay claim to a universal validity or at least an objective intention. But Kant's judgment of taste, spiritualized and lifted onto metaphysical heights, was hardly that of eighteenth-century reality.

In terms of the history of criticism, literary, artistic, and musical, there were no Kantian aesthetic observers in the eighteenth century. The history of arts, letters, and music in the course of the century can be and was written as a series of quarrels. Voltaire was unfair to Fréron, who was unfair to Voltaire, who was unfair to Rousseau, who was unfair to Rameau, who was unfair to Grimm, who was unfair to Palissot, who was unfair to Diderot, who was unfair to Boucher, Van Loo, La Grenée, and the Comte de Caylus, who was unfair to the philosophes, who were unfair to anyone not of their own party. On stage, plays did not always succeed or fail on their intrinsic merits, but were cheered on or put down by claques. In the art exhibitions at the Salon of the Louvre, the placement of a picture might count for or against it. As Du Bos saw, the judgment of taste may well have been a question of class, or from our perspective a question of history. Kant, in any case, published at just the right time: when, as such critics as Quatremère and later Hegel saw, art was dead. The term *aesthetic art* signals precisely that something in the arts and in society was quite different now from the way it had been before.

One might suppose that Kant's formulation of the aesthetic judgment was in harmony with Winckelmann's aestheticism. But was Winckelmann's love of Greek beauty free of desire, or was it his particular desire projected onto Greek beauty? Were collectors free of desire? And if not free of desire, were they ipso facto incapable of sound judgment as to the beauty, authenticity, value, and historical place of the objects they collected? It is and was quite possible to be a lover of the arts, animated by desire, and at the same time a lucid judge of a piece. Most art produced in the course of the eighteenth century, like most literature, was thought of either in moral, utilitarian, passionate terms, or as luxury, baubles, amusements, and pleasures—but hardly as "aesthetic art." If taste could have been pure and free of desire, if it had been the taste of angels, who would have applauded, wept, sighed, hissed, or slept at plays, been ravished by music or bored by a recitative? The more one ponders the Kantian requirement of a purity of judgment free of desire, the more it may be assumed to be a purely ideal judgment, not operative and not expected to be operative in the real world where art was produced in a politically, religiously, and socially charged present. In truth there did exist such works in the eighteenth century, free of associations with the present, namely the Greek and Roman works Winckelmann and others swooned over in a most un-Kantian manner. Had these supposedly perfect works been susceptible of being given sensations, like Condillac's famous hypothetical statue, they might conceivably have exercised a pure, disinterested judgment of taste, free of desire and metaphysically correct. They were certainly used in that manner by those who loved and admired them. Their assumed purity was used to judge the impure arts of the present, the despised Baroque and Rococo.

Kant's aesthetics do not so much sum up the realities of the eighteenth century as point the way to the discourse of the nineteenth century on the arts. Thence the justification of the bourgeois love of art in the abstract, in museums, and its separation from life and work and pleasure and of course pecuniary valuation—all on the level of theory and discourse, while the art market continued to thrive. Beauty was priceless, but it could be sold. Given the aesthetic realm as something or somewhere or some condition or system of thought beyond the rational and the practical, the man of taste could also be lifted, thanks to the new formulation of aesthetic judgment, onto the realm of the ideal. Before him lay a great future in the role of dandy, artist, and aesthete—from Beau Brummel to Oscar Wilde to Tom Wolfe in his impeccable white suit. As the man of taste had been opposed to economic man by the eighteenth century, so would the nineteenth oppose the dandy to the philistine.

Kant came at the right time. Art, which before 1789 and the new society had been inseparable from rank, fortune, passion, desire, pleasure, and luxury, could now assume an identity of its own that could be justified on the theoretical level. For the signs of the past, ancient, medieval, and baroque, having already been distinguished from luxury, were now headed for collections and museums. Their former meaning was and is no longer operative; they have been decontextualized by history and metaphysics. The fan of a duchess, the portrait of a marquis, the image of a saint, the glorious victory picture of a prince or great soldier, like the snuffbox of some fop or the dressing table of the duchess, have ceased to be signs of rank, belief, values, or taste. The fan has become either a memento or an artwork by a famous flower painter. The portrait turns out to have been a genuine Largillière and as such is worth a fortune. The saint, an authenticated Jouvenet, is a fine example of late baroque religious painting and worthy of a museum. The dressing table, by Carlin and once the property of the countess of so-and-so, would fetch another fortune. What had been useful became beautiful; what had been part of experience and rank and belief and decor could now be safely transformed into aesthetic art, as history and theory provided the proper aesthetic distancing. And because all these things were gone forever, and because the beautiful was joined to aesthetic judgment, art could become the object of the cult of the beautiful—beyond history, beyond the passions of baroque culture and the frivolity of the Rococo, and beyond luxury, in a realm of the imagination where the Baroque has become a *je ne sais quoi* bewitching the mind.

Bibliography

Primary Sources

Baudeau, abbé Nicolas. *Explication du tableau économique*. Paris, 1776.

Baudrillart, Henri. *Histoire du luxe public et privé depuis l'antiquité jusqu'à nos jours*. 4 vols. Paris, 1878–82.

Beaumarchais, Pierre-Augustin Caron de. *Le Mariage de Figaro*. In *Oeuvres*. (Gallimard ed.) Paris, 1988.

Blondel, Jacques-François. *L'Homme du monde éclairé par les arts*. 2 vols. Amsterdam and Paris, 1774.

Chastellux, François-Jean, marquis de. *De la félicité publique*. 2 vols. Amsterdam, 1774.

Court de Gébelin, Antoine. *Le Monde primitif*. 9 vols. Paris, 1773–83.

Diderot, Denis. *Essais sur la peinture*. In *Oeuvres esthétiques*. (Garnier ed.) Paris, 1968.

———. *Le Neveu de Rameau*. Paris, 1957.

———. *Le Rêve de d'Alembert*. Paris, 1957.

———. *Le Salon de 1767*. Vol. 3 of *Salons*. Oxford, 1963.

Domat, Jean. *Droit public*. Paris, 1697.

Du Bos, Jean-Baptiste. *Réflexions critiques sur la poésie et la peinture*. (1719.) 7th edition, 1770; rpt. Geneva, 1967.

Dupont de Nemours, Pierre Samuel. "Du principe commun à tous les beaux-arts et de leurs rapports avec l'utilité publique." In *Les Ephémérides du citoyen*, 6:44–45. Paris, 1771.

———. *Lettres à la Margravine Caroline-Louise de Bade sur les salons de 1773, 1777, 1779,* ed. Karl Olsen, Gaston Brière, and Maurice Tourneux. Paris, 1909.

Epinay, Louise de la Live d'. *Histoire de Madame de Montbrillant.* Paris, 1989.

Girardin, René-Louis, marquis de. *De la composition des paysages.* Paris, 1777.

Graffigny, Françoise de. *Lettres d'une Péruvienne.* Paris, 1752.

Helvétius, Claude Adrien. *De l'esprit.* In *Oeuvres complètes,* vols. 1–2. Paris, 1795.

———. *De l'homme.* In *Oeuvres complètes,* vols. 3–4. Paris, 1795.

Hogarth, William. *The Rake's Progress.* London, 1735.

Holbach, Paul Henri Dietrich, baron d'. *Politique naturelle.* London, 1773. In *D'Holbach portatif.* Paris, 1967.

Hume, David. *Essays Moral, Political, and Literary.* Vol. 1. London, 1753.

Kant, Immanuel. *Critique of Judgment.* (1790.) Trans. J.H. Bernard. New York, 1951.

La Bruyère, Jean de. *Caractères.* Paris, 1951.

Lacombe. *Poétique de Voltaire.* Geneva, 1766.

LaFont de Saint-Yenne. *Réflexions sur quelques causes de l'état présent de la peinture en France.* Paris, 1747.

Laugier, Abbé. *Essai sur l'architecture.* Paris, 1753.

Le Camus de Mézières, Nicolas. *Génie de l'architecture.* Paris, 1782.

Ledoux, Claude Nicolas. *L'Architecture considérée sous le rapport de l'art, des moeurs, et de la législation.* Paris, 1802.

Le Gros, Joseph-Marie. *Analyse des ouvrages de Jean-Jacques Rousseau et de Court de Gébelin.* Geneva, 1784.

Le Maître de Claville, Charles-François. *Traité du vrai mérite de l'homme.* 7th ed. Amsterdam, 1741.

Le Mercier de la Rivière, Paul-Pierre. *L'Ordre naturel et essentiel des sociétés politiques.* 2 vols. London, 1767.

Mandeville, Bernard. *The Fable of the Bees, or Private Vices, Public Benefits.* (1714.) New York, 1962.

"Maximes générales du gouvernement agricole le plus avantageux au genre humain." In *L'Espion anglais,* 1:303. Paris, 1779.

Mercier, Louis Sébastien. *L'An 2440, ou rêve s'il en fut jamais.* London, 1771.

———. *Le Nouveau Paris.* Brunswick, 1800.

———. *Tableau de Paris.* 12 vols. Amsterdam, 1782–88.

Mirabeau, Victor Riqueti, marquis de. *L'Ami des hommes, ou Traité de la population.* 2 vols. Avignon, 1756.

———. *Leçons économiques.* Amsterdam, 1770.

Montesquieu, baron de La Brède et de. *L'Esprit des lois.* (1748.) Trans. Thomas Nugent as *The Spirit of Laws.* New York, 1949.

―――. *Lettres persanes.* Cologne, 1721.

Morellet, André. *Mémoires.* 2 vols. Paris, 1818.

Necker, Jacques. *Compte rendu au Roy.* Paris, 1781.

Pascal, Blaise, *Pensées.* Paris, 1964.

Pauw, Corneille de. *Recherches philosophiques sur les Egyptiens et les Chinois.* Berlin, 1753.

Pidansat de Mairobert, Mathieu-François. "Lettres sur les Economistes." In *L'Espion anglais,* 1:275–319. London, 1779.

Pluche, Abbé. *Histoire du ciel.* The Hague, 1741.

Prévost d'Exiles, abbé Antoine François. *Manon Lescaut.* (1733.) Paris, 1965.

Quesnay, François. *Essai physique sur l'économie animale.* Paris, 1736.

―――. *Philosophie rurale, ou économie générale et politique de l'agriculture, réduite à l'ordre immuable des loix physiques et morales, qui assurent la prospérité des empires.* Amsterdam, 1763.

―――. *Tableau économique.* Paris, 1758.

Restif de la Bretonne. *Les Contemporaines par gradation.* 1783–85.

Reynolds, Joshua. *The Discourses of Sir Joshua Reynolds.* London, 1884.

Rousseau, Jean-Jacques. *Les Confessions.* (Pléiade ed.) Paris, 1959.

―――. *Discours.* In *Oeuvres complètes,* vol. 3. (Pléiade ed.) Paris, 1964.

―――. *Emile.* Paris, 1966.

―――. *La Nouvelle Héloïse.* Paris, 1967.

―――. *Rêveries du promeneur solitaire.* Paris, 1959.

Scudéry, Madeleine de. *La Promenade de Versailles.* Paris, 1669.

Sénac de Meilhan, Gabriel. *Considérations sur les richesses et le luxe.* Paris, 1787.

Shaftesbury, Anthony Ashley Cooper, third earl of. *Characteristics of Men, Manners, Opinions, Times.* (1711.) Indianapolis, 1964.

Sieyès, Emmanuel Joseph. *Qu'est-ce que le Tiers Etat?* (1788.) Classiques de la Pensée Politique, 6. Geneve, 1970.

Smith, Adam. *The Theory of Moral Sentiments.* (1759.) Oxford, 1976.

―――. *The Wealth of Nations.* Brussels, 1776.

Viel de Saint-Maux, Jean-Louis. *Lettres sur l'architecture des anciens et celle des modernes.* Brussels, 1779–87.

Volney, Constantin-François, comte de. *Les Ruines, ou méditations sur les révolutions des empires.* Paris, 1791.

Voltaire. *Candide, ou l'optimisme.* (1759.) Trans. Richard Aldington in *The Portable Voltaire,* ed. Ben Ray Redman. New York, 1963.

Secondary Sources

Autin, Jean. *Louis XIV architecte.* Paris, 1981.

Badez, Jean-Michel. *Les Ecrivains et la musique au XVIIIe siècle, III: Philosophes, encyclopédistes, musiciens, théoriciens.* Geneva, 1980.

Beaussant, Philippe. *Rameau de A à Z.* Paris, 1983.

———. *Versailles, opéra.* Paris, 1981.

Bénabou, Erica-Marie. *La Prostitution et la police des moeurs au XVIIIe siècle.* Paris, 1987.

Bonnet, Jean-Claude. *La Carmagnole des muses: L'Homme de lettres et l'artiste dans la Révolution.* Paris, 1988.

Bousquet, Jacques. *Le XVIIIe Siècle romantique.* Paris, 1972.

Braham, Allan. *The Architecture of the French Enlightenment.* Berkeley, 1980.

Campbell, Colin. *The Romantic Ethic and the Spirit of Modern Consumerism.* Oxford, 1987.

Canon, John. *Aristocratic Century: The Peerage of Eighteenth-Century England.* Cambridge, England, 1987.

Charpentrat, Pierre. *Le Mirage baroque.* Paris, 1967.

Chaussinand-Nogaret, Guy. *Gens de finance au XVIIIe siècle.* Paris, 1972.

———. *La Noblesse au XVIIIe siècle.* Paris, 1976.

Cioranescu, Alexandre. *Le Masque et le visage: Du baroque espagnol au classicisme français.* Geneva, 1983.

Corvisier, André. *Arts et sociétés dans l'Europe du XVIIIe siècle.* Paris, 1978.

Crow, Thomas E. *Painters and Public Life in Eighteenth-Century Paris.* New Haven, 1985.

Darnton, Robert. *The Literary Underground in the Old Regime.* Cambridge, Mass., 1982.

Dessert, Daniel. *Argent, pouvoir et société au Grand Siècle.* Paris, 1984.

Didier, Béatrice. *La Musique des lumières.* Paris, 1985.

Diesbach, Ghislain de. *Necker, ou, la faillite de la vertu.* Paris, 1978.

Durand, Yves. *Les Fermiers-généraux au XVIIIe siècle.* Paris, 1971.

Elias, Norbert. *La Société de cour.* Paris, 1974.

Faure, Edgar. *La Banqueroute de Law*. Paris, 1977.

Fernandez, Dominique. *L'Ecole du sud*. Paris, 1991.

Ferrier-Caverivière, Nicole. *Le Grand Roi à l'aube des lumières, 1715–1751*. Paris, 1985.

Gallet, Michel. *Paris Domestic Architecture of the Eighteenth Century*. London, 1972.

Gignoux, C. J. *Turgot*. Paris, 1945.

Goblot, Edmond. *La Barrière et le niveau: Etude sociologique sur la bourgeoisie française moderne*. Paris, 1925.

Goldsmith, M.W. *Private Vices, Public Benefits*. Cambridge, 1985.

Grange, Henri. *Les Idées de Necker*. Paris, 1974.

Groethuysen, Bernard. *Les Origines de l'esprit bourgeois en France*. Paris, 1956.

Kintzler, Catherine. *Jean-Philippe Rameau: Splendeur et naufrage de l'esthétique du plaisir à l'âge classique*. Paris, 1983.

Kirsch, Doris. *La Bruyère, ou le style cruel*. Montreal, 1977.

Lapham, Lewis H. *Money and Class in America: Notes and Observations on Our Civil Religion*. New York, 1988.

Lüthy, Herbert. *La Banque protestante en France de la révocation de l'Edit de Nantes à la Révolution*. 2 vols. Paris, 1959.

———. *From Calvin to Rousseau*. New York, 1970.

Mantion, Jean-Rémy. "Déroutes de l'art: La Destination de l'oeuvre d'art et le débat sur le musée." In *La Carmagnole des muses: L'Homme de lettres et l'artiste dans la Révolution*, ed. Jean-Claude Bonnet, 97–129. Paris, 1988.

Maravall, José Antonio. *Culture of the Baroque*. Minneapolis, 1986.

Mely, Benoit. *Jean-Jacques Rousseau: Un Intellectuel en rupture*. Paris, 1985.

Miller, James. *Rousseau: Dreamer of Democracy*. New Haven, 1984.

Monro, Hector. *The Ambivalence of Bernard Mandeville*. Oxford, 1975.

Myers, Milton L. *The Soul of Modern Economic Man: Ideas of Self-Interest, Thomas Hobbes to Adam Smith*. Chicago, 1983.

Niebelschutz, Wolf von. *Über Barock and Rokoko*. Frankfurt am Main, 1981.

Pomian, Krzysztof. *Collectionneurs, amateurs et curieux: Paris, Venise, XVI–XVIII siècles*. Paris, 1987.

Reddy, William M. *Money and Liberty in Modern Europe: A Critique of Historical Understanding*. Cambridge, England, 1987.

Roche, Daniel. *La Culture des apparences: Une Histoire du vêtement*. Paris, 1989.

Ryan, Alan. *Property and Political Theory*. Oxford, 1984.

Rykwert, Joseph. *The First Moderns: The Architects of the Eighteenth Century*. Cambridge, Mass., 1980.

Skrine, Peter N. *The Baroque*. London, 1978.

Sombart, Werner. *Le Bourgeois: contribution à l'histoire morale et intellectuelle de l'homme économique moderne*. Paris, 1926.

———. *Luxury and Capitalism*. Ann Arbor, Mich., 1967.

Steegman, John. *The Rule of Taste, from George I to George IV*. London, 1936.

Thirion, Henri. *La Vie privée des financiers au XVIIIᵉ siècle*. Paris, 1895.

Veblen, Thorstein. *The Theory of the Leisure Class*. New York, 1899.

Verlet, Pierre. *Le Château de Versailles*. Paris, 1985.

Weulersse, Georges. *La Physiocratie à la fin du règne de Louis XV, 1770–1774*. Paris, 1959.

Williams, Rosalind H. *Dream Worlds: Mass Consumption in Late Nineteenth-Century France*. Berkeley, 1982.

Index

Compositor: Braun–Brumfield, Inc.
      Text: 10/12 Bembo
   Display: Bembo
   Printer: Braun–Brumfield, Inc.
    Binder: Braun–Brumfield, Inc.